Relations

RELATIONS

new & selected poems

EAMON GRENNAN

Graywolf Press

ST. PAUL, MINNESOTA

Publication of this volume is made possible in part by a grant provided by the
Minnesota State Arts Board through an appropriation by the Minnesota State
Legislature, and by a grant from the National Endowment for the Arts.
Significant support has also been provided by Dayton's, Mervyn's, and Target
stores through the Dayton Hudson Foundation, the Bush Foundation, the
Andrew W. Mellon Foundation, the McKnight Foundation, the General Mills
Foundation, the St. Paul Companies, and other generous contributions
from foundations, corporations, and individuals. To these organizations and
individuals we offer our heartfelt thanks.

Published by
Graywolf Press
2402 University Avenue, Suite 203
Saint Paul, Minnesota 55114
All rights reserved.

www.graywolfpress.org

Published in the United States of America

ISBN 1-55597-280-2

2 4 6 8 9 7 5 3 1
First Graywolf Printing, 1998

Library of Congress Catalog Card Number: 98-84456

Cover design: Jeanne Lee

Cover art: Master of the Vyšší Brod (Hohenfurth) Altarpiece,
"Agony in the Garden," detail, Vyšší Brod Altarpiece, Prague,
circa 1350, National Gallery in Prague

Contents

Selected Poems (1978–1993)

from *So It Goes*

FOUR

New Poems (1993–1995)

For My Friends

Selected Poems 1978–1993

*. . . As you probably know it is very hot in the desert, and water is scarce.
How does the Craspaharah Crab get water? It lives in a cave dug out of the
sand with its tail. It piles some small stones outside the mouth of the cave.
During the night the warm air from the cave meets the cold air from outside
and it condenses. The drops of water fall onto the rocks and in the morning
it has something to drink!*

FROM A CHILD'S NOTEBOOK

*The large-leaved day grows rapidly,
And opens in this familiar spot
Its unfamiliar, difficult fern,
Pushing and pushing red after red.*

WALLACE STEVENS, "THE RED FERN"

ONE

Facts of Life, Ballymoney

I would like to let things be:

The rain comes down on the roof
The small birds come to the feeder
The waves come slowly up the strand.

Three sounds to measure
My hour here at the window:
The slow swish of the sea
The squeak of hungry birds
The quick ticking of rain.

Then of course there are the trees—
Bare for the most part.
The grass wide open to the rain
Clouds accumulating over the sea
The water rising and falling and rising
Herring-gulls bobbing on the water.

They are killing cuttlefish out there,
One at a time without fuss.
With a brisk little shake of the head
They rinse their lethal beaks.

Rain-swollen, the small stream
Twists between slippery rocks.
That's all there's to it, spilling
Its own sound onto the sand.

In one breath one wink all this
Melts to an element in my blood.
And still it's possible to go on

Simply living
As if nothing had happened.

Nothing has happened:
Rain inching down the window,
Me looking out at the rain.

A Gentle Art

for my mother

I've been learning how to light a fire
Again, after thirty years. Begin (she'd say)
With a bed of yesterday's newspapers—
Disasters, weddings, births and deaths,
All that everyday black and white of
History is first to go up in smoke. The sticks
Crosswise, holding in their dry heads
Memories of detonating blossom, leaf. Saved
From the ashes of last night's fire,
Arrange the cinders among the sticks.
Crown them with coal nuggets, handling
Such antiquity as behooves it,
For out of this darkness, light. Look,
It's a cold but comely thing
I've put together as my mother showed me,
Down to sweeping the fireplace clean. Lit,
You must cover from view, let it concentrate—
Some things being better done in secret.
Pretend another interest, but never
Let it slip your mind: know its breathing,
Its gulps and little gasps, its silence
And satisfied whispers, its lapping air.
At a certain moment you may be sure (she'd say)
It's caught. Then simply leave it be:
It's on its own now, leading its mysterious
Hungry life, becoming more itself by the minute,
Like a child grown up, growing strange.

Muse, Maybe

You are never at home with her.
Private, she shies the familiar touch.
Lady of half-lights,
You cannot make her out from shadows.

There's no catching up with her:
She sleeps near your sleep.
Your mind wears her face like a mask.
She is the lady of changes.

She's the girl you kissed in the graveyard,
Hers the warm skin under a raincoat.
You turned sixteen that winter, speechless
At heart, for all your speeches.

She wears the air of what's possible,
Making your pulse ache. *Find me out,*
She says. *Put me in the clear.*
You've made such promises before.

In the National Gallery, London

for Derek Mahon

These Dutchmen are in certain touch
With the world we walk on. Velvet
And solid as summer, their chestnut cows
Repeat cloud contours, lie of the land.

Everything gathers the light in its fashion:
That boat's ribbed bulging, the ripple
Of red tweed at the oarsman's shoulder,
The way wood displaces water, how water
Sheens still, the colour of pale irises.

See how your eye enters this avenue
Of tall, green-tufted, spinal trees:
You tense to the knuckled ruts, nod
To the blunted huntsman and his dog,
A farmer tying vines, that discreet couple
Caught in conversation at a barn's brown angle.
You enter the fellowship of laundered light.

From the ritual conducted around this table
These men in black stare coolly back at you,
Their business, a wine contract, done with.
And on brightly polished ice, these villagers

Are bound to one another by the bleak
Intimacies of winter light—a surface
Laid open like a book, where they flock
Festive and desperate as birds of passage
Between seasons, knowing that enclosing sky
Like the back of their hands, at home
In the cold, making no bones of it.

Swifts over Dublin

Stop, look up, and welcome these
Artful dodgers, high-flyers on the wing,
These ecstatic swirlers, sons of air
And daring, daughters of the slow burn,
Who twist and kiss and veer, high
As kites on homecoming. Survivors,

They've put their night-sweats by,
Harrowing darkness in a rumour of wings
And companionable squeaking, riding the blast.
And now, how they celebrate a comeback, casting
High-pitched benedictions down
On shopping centres, stray dogs, monoxide traffic.

From any point of view
They are beyond me, dark sparks of mystery
I must look up to, where they usher
The full flush of summer in, highly
Delighted with themselves and sporting
Their keen, seasonal dominion.

On a 3½ oz. Lesser Yellowlegs, Departed Boston August 28, Shot Martinique September 3

for Phoebe Palmer

Little brother, would I could
Make it so far, the whole globe
Curling to the quick of your wing.

You leave our minds lagging
With no word for this gallant
Fly-by-night, blind flight.

But ah, the shot: you clot
In a cloud of feathers, drop
Dead in a nest of text-books.

Now seasons migrate without you
Flying south. At the gunman's door
The sea-grapes plump and darken.

Tower House, Ballymoney, 1978

1. *Wife*

It is Spring and he brings me wildflowers:
Primroses, bluebells, forget-me-nots.
He stands them in a glass on the kitchen table:
Celandine, stitchwort, violet, ramson.
Their names make a tiny brightness:
Bright young things, they shine,
They shine for days.

I tidy his room and his table.
I rinse the shit from our child's pyjamas.
I boil rice and potatoes and porridge.
He gives me the glittering names of birds:
Wheatear, blackcap, yellowhammer, wren.
In the wind I hang out our washing:
How his shirts dance, standing on their heads.

I move from room to room with brush and dustpan:
The light, when it's not raining,
Trails me like a child around every corner.
Behind the door he's closed, I know
He is staring out his window at the clouds.
I scrape the cold ashes from the grate:
I get the new fire going.

2. *Mother and Child*
  (for Joan)

You form a warm nest for him
Where he creeps in each morning
I'm away. Content, he curls up
Near your heat, and you slip
Head-first into sleep again,

Knowing well what you've made flesh
Of your flesh, of your bone, bone.

You drift between dreams.
You see his red hair shining
Over the book he has propped
Upright against the mound of hip
And stretch of thigh. Early light
Finds your dark head on the pillow,
Whitens the bony wing of his arm.

All day I've carried it around
Just so, like an old photograph:
The vaulted warmth of your body lifting
And letting gently fall the bedclothes,
Light beginning to bloom in his hair.
How his grave eyes slide across the page
Slowly, like loving hands.

3. *Kids, Cat: A Memory for Kate and Conor*

Once on a sea-slapped winter's day, the east wind
Flinging clamorous surf on sand, we took a walk
Without you. Coming back, at the bend
Above the big fire-berried buckthorn tree
Where the house came into view, we caught
The heart-flipping sight of two tiny figures
In yellow slickers and red wellingtons
Edging along the head of land that plunged
From behind the back garden to the beach,
Following our black cat, Lucky. While Joan
Sprinted for the top of the path, I dashed
Towards the rocks you'd have been dashed on
If you stumbled and tumbled down. But, even running,
I could see the great care with which you both
Were doing this, your absolute bent attention

On every step, the way you stretched hands to help
Over humps of rough ground or a sharp rock,
Intending to make your way down by ledges
To the strand, and I remember being amazed
By the daring of it all, then feeling sweet relief
When I stood under you, and your mother was slowly
Shepherding you down—the cat, nimble as a cat,
Leading the way—and slowly on your own feet down
Until one at a time you could jump to my arms
And be safely grounded.
                              All the way home, then,
To our towered house, you kept us two—your glad
Parents—bemused and happy at the tale of how
You'd helped each other into proper gear, gone out
To the garden, taken your bearings and the cat
And set off to find us, who'd left you safe, we thought,
Playing in the cosy bedroom where, night after night—
Hearing the wind from Wales boom in the chimney—
We'd tuck you in, and I'd ask a dozen times from the door
Are you sure you're warm enough now? You're sure?
Until, muffle-tongued, you'd drive me from the room
And that house of ours would settle down at last
Under a sky of bright, storm-beaten stars,
And around that small family, safe for the night.

Sunday Morning through Binoculars

Balmy as summer. It won't last.
The wind is idling somewhere
Out to sea, making its mind up.
No bells. Silence is a state of grace.
From here the farmers' cottages
Are barnacles, limewhite,
Jutting from the lumpy, plum-blue hill.
For once the birds seem unwary, careless:
Meadow pipits foam out of the furze,
A lark plummets into dead heather,
Two twites perch on a grey shoulder
Of limestone. Their tiny mouths
Open and close. I suppose they're singing.
Four black, white-headed cows
Roam in slow fat lazy waves
Over the spongy green shallows
Of their pasture. In the distance
Two boys stand knee-deep
In a platinum pond, skimming stones.
Their motions slow, deliberate as dreams.
I can't hear the stones slap water,
The water hissing, their fox-red dog's
Ecstatic barking. They step now
Gently from the water backwards
And turn to go. The Sabbath
Winking on drenched wellingtons.

Common Theme

1. *Vigil*

I know nothing

Pale wasted flesh
Perplexed
And shivering from us
As spring fattens the grass
Outside his window

Remember
Last thing at night
Winter nights
Steam coiling
From the kettle's beak
Pungency of cloves
Honey and hot whiskey
Chime of the spoon
Striking glass

Now his nose sharp as a nib
Milky glaze of his eyes
A drunken look
The drugs they give him

Remember
His late key at last
Fumbling in the lock
Dull clunk of the bolt
On the kitchen door
The muffled downstairs voices
Rising and falling
In my shiver of dark

Here are his arms
Out at elbow
A heron's bony
Broken wings

Remember
The morning after
Stillness of the house
Miracle smells
Of Sunday breakfast
Sandpaper cough
The lavatory torrent
His footsteps
A tap splashing

Here is the half
Glass of water
He inches to his lips
My hand in silence
Guiding his hand

Remember the Sunday
Cut-crystal glasses
Foaming
With red lemonade
The jug of clear water
Poised above the measure
Of whiskey in his fist
The splash of light

Here
Are his bleached hands
Fumbling with the sheet
Like beached starfish

2. *He Sleeps*

Into the ward slips dusk
Like a dedicated matron
While across the deserted golf-course
A grey mist grows
Luminous among the shadowy
Stark uprights of trees
And beige craters of sand—
     like dawn I imagine
     coming up in China.

3. *Leaving*

Among other things the bed
The bathroom mirror
The clock humming on the mantlepiece
Spectacles winking on the windowsill
Car keys in a pewter ashtray—
Souvenir of Penn. State U.

And outside in his walled garden
A conflagration of daffodils
One amputated apple tree
A tenebrous bush of spring broom
Just beginning to dazzle
And roofing the whole thing in as usual
The perpetual tent of cloud
Tattered with seacoast mountain light

When it comes to flesh and blood
The most fragile things in the world
Are hard as nails

And sit there like stone creatures
Deaf and blind in a silent room
In a silent room and take no notice
When one—as he did—takes his leave

Dublin, March 1981

Laundromat

In the dryer, shaken sleepers,
their washing revives,

Spirals like kites
Flaring fabulous tails.

Sheets belly high spirits,
In love with shirts

Whose empty arms embrace anything:
Hold me, they hopelessly cry,

Wrapped up in one another
Let us never part. They part

Breathless and headlong.
They shine like morning.

Socks, footloose and airy,
Perform prodigies of speed,

Denims tangle with corduroys,
Their wild legs bucking.

Like herons the bath-towels
Flap gravely round. Handkerchiefs

Flutter like finches
Panicky at the feeder

Till their spinning sphere
Slows down, slows down, and stops.

With cold slow hands
He slaps down flat

His wife's underthings: panties,
Bras, a crinkled slip.

She beats his limp jeans
Into manageable squares. They both

Tug tousled sheets straight
And soberly fold them,

Then lay all neatly out
In a plastic yellow basket

Barred as any cage.

Lying Low

The dead rabbit's
Raspberry belly
Gapes like a mouth.

Bees and gilded flies
Make the pulpy flesh
Hum and squirm:

O love, they sing
In their nail-file voices,
We are becoming one another.

His head intact, tranquil,
As if he's dreaming
the mesmerised love of strangers

Who inhabit the red tent
Of his ribs, the radiant
Open house of his heart.

End of Winter

I spent the morning my father died
Catching flies. They'd buzz and hum
Against the warm illuminated pane
Of the living-room window. Breathless,
My hand would butterfly behind them
And cup their fear in my fist,
Their filament wings tickling
The soft centre of my palm. With my
Left hand I unlatched the window
And opened my right wide in the sunshine.
They'd spin for a second like stunned
Ballerinas, then off with them, tiny
Hearts rattling like dice, recovered
From the fright of their lives. I watch
Each one spiral the astonishing
Green world of grass, and drift
Between the grey branches of the ash.
I see each quick dark shadow
Smudge the rinsed and springing earth
That shone beyond belief all morning.
There must have been at least a dozen
I saved like that with my own hands
Through the morning, when they shook off sleep
In every corner of the living room.

Cavalier and Smiling Girl

(Vermeer)

The Old World geography
Of their proximate bodies
Odysseys beyond the actual
Map and gaping window:
They have discovered one another.

Ordinary water glistens
Where her linked fingers
Follow the curve of the glass:
This, she knows, is something
Elemental to hold onto.

Here is heart's cartography
Toying with absence,
Making of great space
A shapely consolation—
A picture of projected grief.

No grief in this luminous
Mortal minute, this little room
Where her indigenous smile
Fixes something between them—
Making light of her life.

Skunk

Night brims with his bittersweet.
Sometimes a squashed body does it: for miles
The highway blows his grief among the trees.

Other times it's fear that burns that incense
In the dark. Or it could be just delight:
Two of them finding one another
Slow and curious
Among moist ferns and cool bluegreen shadows.
Black and white, warm as saliva,
Infinitely, as such things go, desirable.

Making no secret of what's between them,
They hang their lavish presence on the night,
Scattering anarchy in pungent waves
Through the dark beyond the bedroom window.

Fall

On a still morning, the shallow pond
Is full of kissing: little narcissi—
Sandpiper, sanderling, killdeer, plover—
Dip to their brilliant twins

In the motionless water. Egrets connect
With their own stealthy brightness,
Uncoil slow snake-necks and come
Within an inch of the water's skin

And enter. Unsteady rings ride out
From feathered centres, each bird
Making its presence felt, heartfelt
Quick solidity at the heart of things.

And patiently gazing at themselves
In the mirroring water,
The flowers of the season—
Touch-me-not, loosestrife, forget-me not—

Become lovers
of the clear pool, the crisp morning:
Fragrance of ripe apples in the air;
Savour of honey in the empty mouth.

Vespers

Back they flash at dusk:
Incandescent shards of starlight
Scorching the silent grass.

Hedge-dwelling hungry birds,
Morsels of unimaginable dread
Dashed against the garden's peace.

Desperate the intent wren
Wild-eyed among the rushes
Shaking twilight from his vexed wings

Searches for something, something.
Hightailing it for cover: *Where,*
Where is it? Where is it?

Night Driving in the Desert

Move fluent as water
Splashing brightness. Imagine
Jackal, badger, wild goat,
Fox-eyes glinting like broken glass:
Gingerly they sniff the sour exhaust.

Remember greenness; name
Its distant children: *ryegrass,*
Olive, avocado, fig—
First sweetness welling in the mouth.

Herbs the Arabs call *ashab*
Sprout inside a single rain,
Rush to blossom fruit seed,
Staining the sand with rainbows.

Imagine a procession of tanager dresses
Drifting through plaited shadow:
Women crossing the earth like water,
Sunlight splashing their skin to stars.

I know it is over in a flash and after
My heart is beating wildly, wildly for days.

Winter

Who, when they are all gone,
Will you be to yourself? You swallow air
Like ether edged with razor-blades,
Run squeaking over frozen snow.

Summer was like love and marriage:
You could scarcely see the cold
Coming through a haze of fat grass,
Flesh. You wake and find it's done for.

This weather brings us to our senses:
Pity the fox, the melancholy badger,
The fieldmouse clean as a snowflake,
Shivering and praying in the flayed hedges.

Raeburn's Skater

I want his delicate balance, his
Sturdy, sane, domesticated grace.

Arms crossed, he holds himself together,
Equilibrist of spirit, solid nerve.

Crowblack and solemn he lives at a tilt
Between limegreen ice and coral air.

Beyond his ken, out of the picture,
The fixed stars hold him fast.

For the Record

After six unsparing days of storm
A grey still day without rain.
Nothing spectacular, no exploding
Stars off the lake, no precious
Glitter of soaked grass, no triumph
In bannering branches, just branches
Taking the air as if it belonged
To them, the faint sleepy *Chink-*
Chink of the robin in the next field,
And everything back in its place.
But nothing carnival or sabbatical,
Only a steady domestic peace
Secures all animations in the garden,
Giving everything its due. No fuss,
No unexpected flares, no amazing
Grace in the play and swift trans-
Figurings of light off water. Only
Cloud, seamless still air, this hush.
So, after six days of storm, record
A perfectly ordinary day at last—
Dry, a little on the cool side.

TWO

Wing Road

Amazing, how the young man who empties
our dustbin ascends the truck as it moves
away from him, rises up like an angel
in a china-blue check shirt and lilac
woollen cap, dirty work-gloves, rowanberry
red bandanna flapping at his throat. He plants
one foot above the mudguard, locks
his left hand to a steel bar
stemming from the dumper's loud mouth
and is borne away, light as a cat, right leg
dangling, the dazzled air snatching at that black-
bearded face. He breaks to a smile, leans wide
and takes the morning to his puffed chest,
right arm stretched far out, a checkered china-blue wing
gliding between blurred earth
and heaven, a messenger under the locust trees
that stand in silent panic at his passage. But
his mission is not among the trees: he
has flanked both sunlit rims of Wing Road
with empty dustbins, each lying on its side,
its battered lid fallen beside it, each
letting noonlight scour its emptiness
to shining. Carried off in a sudden cloud
of diesel smoke, a woeful crying out
of brakes and gears, a roaring of monstrous
mechanical appetite, he has left this unlikely
radiance straggled behind him, where the crows,
covening in branches, will flash and haggle.

Incident

for Louis Asekoff

Mid-October, Massachusetts. We drive
through the livid innards of a beast—dragon
or salamander—whose home is fire. The hills
a witch's quilt of goldrust, flushed cinnamon,
wine fever, hectic lemon. After dark,
while water ruffles, salted, in a big pot, we four
gather towards the woodfire, exchanging
lazy sentences, waiting dinner. Sunk
in the supermarket cardboard box,
the four lobsters tip and coolly stroke each other
with rockblue baton legs and tentative
antennae, their breath a wet clicking, the undulant
slow shift of their plated bodies
like the doped drift of patients
in the padded ward. Eyes like squished berries
out on stalks. It's the end of the line
for them, yet faintly in that close-companioned air
they smell the sea, a shadow-haunted hole to hide in
till all this blows over.
                              When it's time,
we turn the music up to nerve us
to it, then take them one by one and drop
in the salty roil and scald, then clamp
the big lid back. Grasping the shapely fantail,
I plunge mine in headfirst and feel
before I can detach myself the flat slap
of a jackknifed back, glimpse for an instant
before I put the lid on it
the rigid backward bow-bend of the whole body
as the brain explodes and lidless eyes
sear white. We two are bound in silence
till the pot-lid planks back and music

floods again, like a tide. Minutes later,
the four of us bend to brittle pink intricate
shells, drawing white sweet flesh
with our fingers, sewing our shroud-talk
tight about us. Later, near moonless midnight,
when I scrape the leafbright broken remains
into the garbage can outside, that last
knowing spasm eels up my arm again
and off, like a flash, across the rueful stars.

Daughter Lying Awake

Absence takes me heartsick
to my father's bony arms:
we make slow circles together.

The spider-plant shines in secret;
ferns fashion a green bedroom
where I dream his goodnight kiss,

living behind closed doors
with my dolls, my deep amazement,
and the strange

sad names of my dolls:
Hope, Heartsease, Love-
Lies-Bleeding.

March: the sharp sunlight
whittles exact shadows,
polishing platinum claws.

Grandfather's dead, he tells me,
sewing a shroud of words.
We'll go away together. Home

is the smell of lamb chops and
apples sweetening the kitchen:
mother's tears between the sheets.

Something is coming into leaf,
staining my window blind green:
nothing can stop that bleeding.

Something is flowing upwards
towards the clear heads of crocuses
like music in the dark.

My daisy, he says,
my buttercup daughter,
eyebright, my wild geranium,

my light mist
in the morning. His music.
I turn my face

to the wall
that's deaf to anything.
I try to sleep.

Traveller

He's ten, travelling alone for the first time—
by bus to the city. He settles an empty seat
and waves out at where I stand on the footpath
waiting for him to be taken, barely a shadow
grinning behind smoked glass. To his eyes
I'm a dim figure far off, smiling and waving
in a sea of traffic. Behind me, the blinding sun
melts down the black back of hills
across the Hudson. For all there is to say
we are deaf to one another
and despatch our love in shrugs and pantomime
until he gives thumbs-up and the bus
sighs shut, shuddering away from me. He mouths
words I can't understand; I smile back
regardless, blowing a kiss through the air that
starts to stretch and empty between us. Alone,
he stares out a while, admiring his height
and speed, then reads two chapters of *The Dark
Is Rising*. When the real dark leaches in
he sees nothing but the huge loom
of a hill, the trees' hooded bulk and
come-hithering shadow. He tries to curl up
in sleep, but sleep won't come, so he presses
one cheek flat against the cold black glass
and peers past his own faint ghost
up at the sky, as any night-time traveller
would—as Henry Hudson must have, sailing
his *Half Moon* past Poughkeepsie, already
smelling the Pacific. My son seeks the stars
he knows: Orion's belt, his sword, his dog
fall into place, make sense of the dark
above his voyaging. *When I found him,* he says,
I felt at home, and fell asleep. I imagine

him asleep in his rocky seat there,
like that wet sea-boy dozing at mast-head,
whose lullaby the whole Atlantic hums
in the lull between storms, the brief
peace between battles, no land in sight.

Porridge

While you're cooking breakfast
I follow the thread of its smell
back to that first kitchen where
porridge bubbled on the aster-
blue petals of gas. Bland and
mealy as flour sacks, the smell
used snake upstairs to where
I find myself, half dressed, shivering
before the electric fire's redgold stems
that buzz in blueberry tiles and glow
like the statue of the Sacred Heart.

Coffeedark was my father's
morning scent, cigarette smoke
and the acrid black of toast
scorching under the grill. The sharp
rasp of his knife scraped burnt bits
off, butter on: a smell of charcoal
mixed with honeyed gold. Tea
was what the rest of us drank: no smell
unless I dipped my head, felt
steam wreathing cold cheeks, my nose
opening with the word *Ceylon*
—delicate as the bone china tea-set
tinted with its applegreen leaf
we used only on Sunday
or for visitors. Sniffing into the cup
like that, I'd picture my mother
bowed above the smoky basin
of Friar's Balsam, madonnaed
by a blue bath-towel, her breathing

a rich mix of phlegm and prayers
for a speedy recovery, the bedroom
a dispensary stew of wintergreen, camphor,
menthol, blackcurrant, Vick's.

If I was up first, I'd cat-pad downstairs
in stocking feet, ease the halldoor open
to bring in the milk I'd heard the milkman
clunk on the porch, empties clinking
at his finger-ends. It was beginning
to brighten: the milk shone white as milk
in its slender bottles, and the *clop clop*
of the milkman's horse, loose harness
jingling, passed up Clareville Road.
Morning smelled frost, a cut-crystal scent
that said another world existed —
clean-cold, intricate as a frozen snowflake,
somehow parallel to ours—hazardous
and dazzling, and moonlit-fixed forever.
Sometimes a fresh olivebrown horseturd
smoked on the empty street like a
burnt offering, its racy breath a summer-
pungent mix of oats and meadowgrass
inflaming our tame suburban air. Frost
stiffened filaments in my nose, crinkled
the leftover roses, salted the lawn, glinted
from the grey pavement. Kitchen smells
seeping from the house behind me, I'd hug
the four cold bottles to my chest,
heel the halldoor shut and hurry
to pour on my porridge the creamy
top of the milk—rich, delicious,
forbidden—before my mother or my father

saw me: smells of sugar, cream, and porridge
marry, and I take that wonder in
like nothing special, till here and now
I hear you tell me from our kitchen
that breakfast's ready, and I rise
to join you, my head swimming.

Staying in Bed

We lay all morning talking. The window
brightens November grey to knife-edge blue where
Sunday becomes itself, all bells, without us. The air
flickers, blinks, riddled with starling shadows
or the brusque impulsive blobs of sparrows
flung by hunger. This one touch of winter
makes us face a few home truths: we have to enter
the cold zone naked. Sleepwalker steady, our slow

voices cross the little space between us.
Companionable, our bodies stretch. Our sex
idles, half asleep, a summer stream
flooding with fernlight green as
early wheat. Such peace: we could be dreaming
away each other's past, digesting hard facts.

Totem

All Souls' over, the roast seeds eaten, I set
on a backporch post our sculpted pumpkin
under the weather, warm still for November.
Night and day it gapes in at us
through the kitchen window, going soft
in the head. Sleepwalker-slow, a black rash of ants
harrows this hollow globe, munching
the pale peach flesh, sucking its seasoned
last juices dry. In a week, when the ants and
humming flies are done, only a hard remorseless light
drills and tenants it through and through. Within,
it turns mould-black in patches, stays
days like this while the weather takes it
in its shifty arms: wide eye-spaces shine,
the disapproving mouth holds firm. Another week,
a sad leap forward: sunk to one side
so an eye-socket's almost blocked, it becomes
a monster of its former self. Human, it would have
rotted beyond unhappiness and horror
to some unspeakable subject state—its nose
no more than a vertical hole, the thin
bridge of amber between nose and mouth
in ruins. The other socket opens
wider than ever: disbelief.
                              It's all downhill
from here: knuckles of sun, peremptory
steady fingers of frost, strain all day and night—
cracking the rind, kneading the knotted fibres
free. The crown, with its top-knot mockery
of stalk, caves in; the skull buckles; the whole
sad head drips tallowy tears: the end
is in sight. In a day or two it topples on itself
like ruined thatch, pus-white drool spidering
from the corner of the mouth, worming its way

down the body-post. All dignity to the winds,
it bows its bogeyman face of dread
to the inevitable.
                          And now, November almost out,
it is in the bright unseasonable sunshine
a simmer of pulp, a slow bake, amber shell speckled
chalk-grey with lichen. Light strikes and strikes
its burst surfaces: it sags, stays at the end of
its brief tether—a helmet of dark circles, death caul.
Here is the last umbilical gasp, everybody's
nightmare parent, the pitiless system
rubbing our noses in it. But pity poor lantern-head
with his lights out, glob by greasy glob
going back where he came from: as each seed-shaped
drop falls free, it catches and clutches
for one split second the light. When the pumpkin
lapses to our common ground at last—where
a swaddle of snow will fold it in no time
from sight—I try to take in the empty space it's left
on top of the wooden post: it is that empty space.

Jewel Box

Your jewel box of white balsa strips
and bleached green Czechoslovakian rushes
stands open where you keep it shelved
in the bathroom. Morning and evening
I see you comb its seawrack tangle of shell,
stone, wood, glass, metal, bone, seed
for the bracelet, earring, necklace, brooch
or ring you need. Here's brass from Nepal,
a bangle of African ivory and chased silver
for your wrist, a twist of polished
sandalwood seeds, deep scarlet,
gleaming like the fossil tears
of some long-gone exotic bird
with ruby crest, sapphire claws. Adriatic
blue, this lapis lazuli disc will brighten
the pale of your throat, and on this small
alabaster seal-ring the phantom of light
inscribes a woman tilting an amphora, clear
as day, almost as old as Alexander. To the
ebony velvet brim of your hat you'll pin
a perfect oval of abalone, a dark-whorled
underwater sheen to lead us to work
this foggy February morning. We'll leave
your nest of brightness in the bathroom
between the mirror and the laundry-basket
where my dirty shirts sprawl like
drunks amongst your skirts and blouses. Lace-
work frills and rainbow silk pastels, your panties
foam over the plastic brim, and on the shower-rail
your beige and talc-white bras dangle by one strap
like the skinned Wicklow rabbits I remember
hanging from hooks outside the victuallers'
big windows. We've been domesticated strangely,
love, according to our lights: when you

walk by me now, naked and not quite dry
from the shower, I flatten my two hands
on your wet flank, and wonder at the tall
column of flesh you are, catching the faint
morning light that polishes you pale as
alabaster. You're warm, and stay a moment
still like that, as though we were two planets
pausing in their separate orbits, pendant,
on the point of crossing. For one pulse-stroke
they take stock of their bodies
before returning to the journey. Dressed,
you select a string of chipped amber
to hang round your neck, a pair of star-shaped
earrings, a simple ring of jet-black
lustrous onyx. Going down the stairs and
out to the fogbound street, you light my way.

Lizards in Sardinia

I miss our lizards. The one who watched us
lunch on the rocks, half of him
sandstone brown, the other half neat rings
of neon avocado. He moved his head
in wary jerks, like a small bird. Unblinking,
his stillness turned him stone. When he
shifted, whiptail, his whole length flowed
like water. Those reptile eyes of his
took in a world we couldn't see, as he paused
in the dragon-roar of sunlight
till his blood boiled again, then lit out for shadows
and an age of fragrance. The other one—
who'd lost his tail and stumped about, still
quick as a lizard—vanishing behind the trunk
of the eucalyptus. Two who scuttled circles,
tail of one clamped fast in the other's mouth:
courtship, you hoped, as they dervished
among the piebald, finger-slim, fallen leaves
and rustled into infinity—a flash,
an absence—minute leftovers with molten brains,
escapees when their sky-high brothers bowed
cloud-scraping heads and bit the dust, leaving
the wrecked armadas of their ribs
for us to wonder at. Or that plump one
I watched for a long time squatting beside me
at the edge of the steel and turquoise bay
you rose from dripping light and smiling
in my direction: unblemished emerald
down half his length, the rest opaque and
dull, we thought, till we saw the envelope
of old skin he was shedding, under which
jewel-bright he blazed our breath away—the image
of the one I dreamt when my father died, big
as an iguana and the colour of greaseproof paper

till I saw him gleam and be a newborn beast
of jade and flame, who stood there mildly casting
his old self off, and shining. Those afternoons
after we'd made love, I lay quite still
along your back, blood simmering, and saw
your splayed palms flatten on the white sheet
like a lizard's, while we listened—barely
breathing—to the wind whiffle the eucalyptus
leaves against the window, our new world
steadying around us, its weather settled.

Song

At her Junior High School graduation,
she sings alone
in front of the lot of us—

her voice soprano, surprising,
almost a woman's. It is
the *Our Father* in French,

the new language
making her strange, out there,
fully fledged and

ready for anything. Sitting
together—her separated
mother and father—we can

hear the racket of traffic
shaking the main streets
of Jersey City as she sings

Deliver us from evil,
and I wonder can she see me
in the dark here, years

from belief, on the edge
of tears. It doesn't matter. She
doesn't miss a beat, keeps

in time, in tune, while into
our common silence I whisper,
Sing, love, sing your heart out!

Soul Music: The Derry Air

A strong drink, hundred-year-old
schnapps, to be sipped at, invading
the secret places that lie in wait and
lonely between bone and muscle, or
counting (Morse code for insomniacs)
the seconds round the heart
when it stutters to itself. Or to be
taken in at the eyes in small doses,
phrase by somatic phrase, a line
of laundry after dawn, air clean as
vodka, snow all over, the laundry
lightly shaking itself from
frigid sleep. Shirts, flowered sheets,
pyjamas, empty trousers, empty
socks—risen as at a last day's dawn
to pure body, light as air. Whiteness
whiter than snow, blueness bluer than
new day brightening the sky-lid
behind trees stripped of their illusions
down to a webbed geometry
subtler than speech. A fierce blue eye
farther off than God, witnessing
house-boxes huddled together
for comfort, that blindly front
the deserted streets down which in time
come farting lorries full of soldiers.
You are a fugitive *I,* a singing
nerve; you flit from garden to garden
in your fit of silence, bits of you
flaking off in steam and sizzling
like hot fat in the snow. Listen
to the pickers and stealers, the shots,
man-shouts, women wailing, the cry of kids
who clutch stuffed dolls or teddy bears

and shiver, gripping tight as a kite
whatever hand is offered. Here
is the light glinting on top-boots, on the
barrel of an M-16 that grins, holding its
hidden breath, beyond argument. And here
is a small room where robust winter sunlight
rummages much of the day when the day
is cloudless, making some ordinary potted plants
flower to your surprise again, again,
and again: pink, anemic red, wax-white
their resurrection petals. Like hearts
drawn by children, like oiled arrowheads,
their unquestioning green leaves seem
alive with expectation.

A Closer Look

for Peter Fallon

Simply that I'm sick of our wars and
the way we live, wasting everything we touch
with our hands, lips, tongues, crowding
the earth with early graves, blind
to the bright little nipples of rain
that simmer on willow twigs, amber shoots
of the stumped willow itself a burning bush
on the scalloped hem of the ice-pond. So
I'm turning to winter beasts instead, their
delicate razor's-edge economies as they
shift for themselves between dens, migrant
homebodies like the souls we used to have,
leaving behind them in the shallow snow
their signatures, the thing itself, illiterate
signs that say no more than *We were here*
and mean it: handprints, footprints, midnight-
mahogany blossoms of shit, citrus and
mustardgreen swirls of piss that brighten
the eye-numbing, one blank world. Porcupine,
possum, raccoon, skunk, fox—behold them
combing the cold land for a bite, not just
taking for granted their world as it comes
and goes. They wear the weather like a shawl,
following their noses through a sphere of
sudden death and instant satisfactions. They lie
in the sunlit pit of sleep, or the worm of hunger
unwinds his luminous tail to rouse and
send them coldly forth, sniffing the wind
the way lovers browse word by word by word
first letters for what stays salted
and aromatic between the lines. It isn't
innocence I find in them, but a fathoming

depth of attention anchored in the heart, its
whorl of blood and muscle beating round—the way
they traffic between frosted starlight
and the gleamy orbs of berries and last apples,
between storm in the big cloud-bearing boughs
and the narrow breath of earthworm and beetle
barely stirring the dead leaves, now all
quivering dash, nerves purring, now the wildfire
flash of pain that lays them, an open secret,
low. I try to make my hopeless own of this,
to sense in myself their calm unthreading
between brisk teeth or busy mycelian fingers,
breaking—as we will—down to our
common ground, the whole story starting over
in the old language: air first, then
ooze, then the solid lie of things, then fire,
a further twist, begin again. Making do.

Men Roofing

for Seamus Heaney

Bright burnished day, they are laying fresh roof down
on Chicago Hall. Tight cylinders of tarred felt-paper
lean against one another on the cracked black shingles
that shroud those undulant ridges. Two squat drums
of tar-mix catch the light. A fat canister of gas
gleams between a heap of old tyres and a paunchy
plastic sack, beer-bottle green. A TV dish-antenna
stands propped to one side, a harvest moon, cocked
to passing satellites and steadfast stars. Gutters
overflow with starlings, lit wings and whistling throats
going like crazy. A plume of blue smoke feathers up
from a pitch-black cauldron, making the air fragrant
and medicinal, as my childhood's was, with tar. Overhead,
against the gentian sky, a sudden first flock whirls
of amber leaves and saffron, quick as breath, fine
as origami birds. Watching from a window opposite,
I see a man in a string vest glance up at these
exalted leaves, kneel to roll a roll of tar-felt flat; another
tilts a drum of tar-mix till a slow bolt of black silk
oozes, spreads. One points a silver hose and conjures
from its nozzle a fretted trembling orange lick
of fire. The fourth one dips to the wrist in the green sack
and scatters two brimming fistfuls of granite grit:
broadcast, the bright grain dazzles on black. They pause,
straighten, study one another: a segment done. I can see
the way the red-bearded one in the string vest grins and
slowly whets his two stained palms along his jeans; I see
the one who cast the grit walk to the roof-edge, look over,
then, with a little lilt of the head, spit contemplatively
down. What a sight between earth and air they are, drenched
in sweat and sunlight, relaxed masters for a moment
of all our elements. Here is my image, given, of the world

at peace: men roofing, taking pains to keep the weather
out, simmering in ripe Indian-summer light, winter
on their deadline minds. Briefly they stand balanced
between our common ground and nobody's sky, then move
again to their appointed tasks and stations, as if they were
amazing strangers, come to visit for a brief spell
our familiar shifty climate of blown leaves, birdspin. Odorous,
their lazuli column of smoke loops up from the dark
heart of their mystery; and they ply, they intercede.

At Home in Winter

1.

We sit across from one another
in front of the fire, the big logs
clicking and hissing. Outside
is bitter chill: locust branches
grow brittle as crystal. You
are sewing a skirt, your pursed mouth
full of pins, head spinning with
Greek and Latin. You frown
so not to swallow any pins
when you try to smile at me
slumped under the *TLS* and bewailing
the seepage of my days, the way
my life runs off like water, yet
inexplicably happy at this moment
balanced between us like a tongue of flame
skiving a pine log and seeming
to breathe, its whole involuntary life
spent giving comfort. It would
be a way to live: nothing
going to waste; such fullness
taking off, warm space;
a fragrance. Now the sight of you
bending to baste the blue skirt
before you pleat and sew the waistband in
enters and opens inside me, so
for a second or two I am an empty centre,
nothing at all,
then back to this home truth
unchanged: you patiently taking
one thing at a time as I can't,
all the while your head beating
with hexameters and foreign habits. I go on

reading in silence, as if I hadn't
been startled into another life
for a fiery instant, inhaling the faintly
resinated air that circulates
like blood between our two bodies.

2.

Blown in from the noonwhite bite of snow
I find the whole house fragrant as a haycock
with the soup you've stirred up, its spirit
seeping into closets, curtains, bedrooms—
a prosperous mix of chicken stock, carrots,
garlic, onion, thyme. All morning
you've wreathed your head in it, and now
you turn to me like a minor deity of earth
and plenty, hands dipped to the wrist
in the flesh of vegetables, your fingers
trailing threads from the mound of bones
glistening on the counter-top. You stand
at the edge of a still life—glazed
twists of onion skin, papery garlic sacs,
bright carrot stumps, grass-green delicate
stems of parsley, that little midden
of bones—and I behold
how in the middle of my daily life
a sober snow-bound house
can turn to spirit of chicken, air
a vegetable soul, and breathe on me. Turning
back to the stove, wooden spoon
still steaming, you say
in no time now we'll sit and eat.

Four Deer

Four deer lift up their lovely heads to me
in the dusk of the golf course I plod across
towards home. They're browsing the wet grass
the snow has left and, statued, stare at me
in deep silence, and I see what light there is
gather to glossy pools in their eight mild,
barely curious but wary eyes. When one at a time
they bend again to feed, I can hear the crisp
moist crunch of the surviving grass
between their teeth, imagine the slow lick of a tongue
over whickering lips. They've come from the unlit
winter corners of their fright to find
a fresh season, this early gift, and stand
almost easy at the edge of white snow islands and
lap the grey-green sweet depleted grass. About them
hangs an air of such domestic sense, the comfortable
hush of folk at home with one another, a familiar
something I sense in spite of the great gulf of strangeness
we must look over at each other. Tails flicker
white in thickening dusk, and I feel their relief at
the touch of cold snow underfoot while their faces
nuzzle grass, as if, like birds, they'd crossed
unspeakable vacant wastes with nothing but hunger
shaping their brains, driving them from leaf to
dry leaf, sour strips of bark, under a thunder of guns
and into the cold comfort of early dark. I've seen
their straight despairing lines cloven in snowfields
under storm, an Indian file of famished natives, poor
unprayed-for wanderers through blinding chill, seasoned
castaways in search of home ports, which they've found
at last, here on winter's verge between our houses and
their trees. All of a sudden, I've come too close. Moving
as one mind they spring in silent waves
over the grass, then crack snow with sharp hard

snaps, lightfooting it into the sanctuary of a pine grove
where they stand looking back at me, a deer-shaped
family of shadows against the darker arch of trees and
this rusting dusk. When silence settles over us again
and they bow down to browse, the sound of grass being
lipped, bitten, meets me across the space between us. Close
enough for comfort, they see we keep, instinctively,
our distance—knowing our place, sharing this air
where a few last shards of daylight still glitter
in little meltpools or spread a skin of brightness
on the ice, the ice stiffening towards midnight
under the clean magnesium burn of a first star.

Morning: The Twenty-second of March

for Rachel

All the green things in the house
on fire with greenness. The trees
in the garden take their naked ease
like *Demoiselles d'Avignon.* We came awake
to the spider-plant's crisp shadow
printing the pillowcase
between us. Limp fingers of steam
curl auspiciously from the cup
of tea I've brought you, and a blue-jay
screeches blue murder beyond the door.
In a painting over the bed
five tea-coloured cows stand
hock-deep in water at the broad
bend of a stream—small smoothback stones
turtling its near margin. A brace
of leafy branches leans over it
from the far bank, where the sun
spreads an open field like butter,
and the cows bend down
to the dumbfound smudge of their own faces
in the flat, metallic water. And here
this minute, at the bristle tip
of the Scotch pine, a cardinal
starts singing: seven compound metal notes
equal in beat, then silence, then
again the identical seven. Between
the sighs the cars and pick-ups make,
relenting for the curve with a little
gasp of gears, we hear over the road
among the faintly flesh pink
limbs and glow of the apple orchard
a solitary dove throating three sweet

mournful *Om*, then falling silent, then
—our life together hesitating in this gap
of silence, slipping from us and becoming
nothing we know in the swirl that has
no past, no future, nothing
but the pure pulse-shroud of light, the dread
here-now—reporting thrice again
its own silence. The cup of tea
still steams between your hands
like some warm offering or other
to the nameless radiant vacancy at the window,
this stillness in which we go on happening.

Conjunctions

1.

In the cold dome of the college observatory
I wait my turn to lay an eye on
Halley's Comet. For a minute I'm a watcher
of the skies in total silence, my whole self
swimming the shaft of the telescope—blunt
as a big gun—out across the dark to our one
and only rendezvous. It's a faint, milky bristling,
like the frizzled head of a small dandelion
gone to seed. Distinctly throbbing, sperm-like and
full of purpose in its journey, it seems as intimate
as the tick of my own pulse, though its far heart is
ice and a rage of lizard-green, sulphur, steel-blue,
its corona cloudy rose, riding into the light
of our world at biblical intervals, a hard fact, a sign
simply *out there,* meaning maybe nothing at all
or just what we make of it. But this once, at least,
I'm here to meet it, make its path cross mine, figuring
the unthinkable winter space between the lot of us—
those impossible distances, and the uncanny, happy,
unrepeatable accident. This is all I see before
I step back into our night glinting with chill
and see the sky an unreadable maze of stars, its sudden
comings and goings—brief white birds ablaze—and
under my boots the snow gleaming, hard as stone.

2.

A hard bright day, late February, you tell me
you're pregnant. The dead grass scabbed with snow
and oozing a premature, deceptive thaw, we cross
at the lights on Raymond, holding hands against
the heavy traffic. You've been sick—your system

briefly poisoned, in a fist of fever by day, nightsweats—
and we worry it will make some dangerous
difference. I imagine this circumstantial creature
taking shape inside you, our quick derivative,
yet already someone separate and strange, a pulse
of difference in the dark uncharted space
you've offered up, a hurried little heartbeat
syncopate with yours, compounding hearts. It's
early days yet, but you've opened my weather eye
for signs—for a warm corner in the ice-wind
rattling last year's locust pods like *maracas,* a
flash of frantic amber in the stark branches
of the willow, a few lemon flecks on the goldfinch,
or a hoarse wheeze from the first redwing blackbird
to claim home ground among the mazy brush and cattails
out back. These live signs will wind around you
like planets, love, while you grow more than yourself
at the season's weathery, fragrant, unprevailing
heart. And on the outskirts I will bend to listen
to that other heart kicking its mysteries—before our
ground and gravity—in the still enlarging dark.

3.

I'm in the dark, going home fast
along the Palisades, the night roaring and flashing
with the cars I pass, that pass me, all our lives at hazard
on the simple spin of a wheel, locked anonymously into
this meteor shower above the legal speed limit. I have
been handing over to Joan the children, as happens
every other week-end: we meet at a gas-station and
deliver our children up—lovingly, to take the sting
out of it—to one another. I'm thinking about this,
about the way my words can't catch it yet but
about must, and about must go—trying to be true
to the unavoidable ache in the grain of healing,

trying to boil the big words down to size—when a fox
lights out of hiding in the highway's grassy island
and arrows across the road before me, a rust-
gold flash from dark to dark. In that split second I catch
the compass-point of his nose, the quilted tip
of ears *in áirde,* the ruddering lift of a tail as he
streams by my sight, and I only have time to
lift my instinct's foot from the gas, clap hands, cry
"Fox!" in fright or invocation and he's gone, under
the metal fence, into the trees, home free. But all
the way home I hold him in my mind: a body
burning to its outer limits of bristle with
this moment, creature eyes alive with purpose, child
of time and impeccable timing
who has cometed across my vacant dark, a flow
of leaf-rust and foxy gold, risk-taker
shooting sure as a bird into the brush
with every hair in place, a splice
of apprehension, absolute, and pure indifference.
He is only getting on with his life, I know,
but engraved on my brain for good now
is his cave shape at full stretch, caught
in the brief blaze of my headlights
just like that . . . and still running.

THREE

Two Climbing

1.

After the blackface sheep, almond coats daubed
to the blush of slaughtered innards,
all I saw going up was a small frog
speckled rust and raw olive, slick
as a lizard, with a lizard's fixed
unblinking eye. It splays and tumbles
to a safe shadow
where heather-roots wind through limestone
while I keep climbing
behind Conor, who's twelve, my heart
starting to knock at thin air, effort. He loves
leading me on, and when I look up
to where he stands waiting—legs apart and
firmly planted on a rock spur, gazing round him
at the mountains and the sea, the thin
ribboning road beige below us, my figure
bent over the flat green hands of bracken—
I'm struck sharp as a heart pain
by the way this minute brims
with the whole story: such touched fullness
and, plain as day, the emptiness at last.

2.

Once down again, safe home, we both
look wondering up to the top of Tully Mountain
and the barely visible concrete plinth
that peaks it, on which he sat
exalted for a time and took
the whole of Ireland in, he said,
with one big swivelling glance, and took twelve snaps
to prove it: a windy shimmer

of cloud, mountain, water—a rack
of amphibian spirits drifting
over our heads. I saw the way our elevation
simplified the lower world
to rocky crops and patches, neat
green and tea-brown trapezoids
of grass and bog, bright pewtered spheres
of pure reflection. We sat out of the wind
on two flat rocks, and passed
in silence to one another
another sweet dry biscuit
and a naggin whiskey bottle
of water, pleased with ourselves
at some dumb male thing for which
he finds the word: *adventure*. Going down,
he lopes, leads, is deliberately solicitous,
pointing out loose rocks, the treacherous
bright green surface
of a swampy passage, a safer way.
Non-stop, his knowing talk
enlarges airily our trek and conquest.

3.

Walking at last the field path
to the house, he is all
straight spine and limber stride
in his mudded wellingtons,
while I note how stone silent
the plum-coloured broad back of the mountain is,
keeping the wind off our lives
in this hollow. Before going in,
he sets on an outside windowsill
the horned sheep skull we've salvaged
from the bracken, weathered to a cracked adze
of jawbone ringed and bristling

with broken teeth. Bone-flanged, the great
eye sockets gape, and like fine stitching
the skull's one partition
seams dead centre. In less than a week from now
he'll have forgotten this bony trophy,
but not the journey we took together
to find it: that hammering brisk ascent, the luminous
view of everything, those buffeting winds, the one
unruffled interlude of quiet, then, in the end,
that sweet leading down. While I'll go on
watching the split skull—colour of crushed almond
or washed-out barley muslin—shine.

Circlings

for Rachel & Kira

The little electric hum of her nerves
under my hand; her lungs
humming our latest air. The garden
a bed of dead leaves
where a young bird is born again
out of the cat's soft jaws. Milkblue,
the two eyes shine in her head.

Singing her hundred words for milk
she takes our noiseworld in. But what
in the marvelling moment's
span of her attention
can she make of the frost feathers
glinting in the bedroom window
or the single fish-eye of light, olive-yellow,
swimming in oil in the slim bottle
after her bath? My face
floats down—a spiked cloud
of flesh and freckles, a sphere
of hairy thunder. My hand
is a sea anemone
in a pool of air, my crook'd finger
a shy beast brushing something
she can feel she feels.

In the corner under a nightlight
you sit in the rocking-chair
feeding the baby. From my pillow
I see the shadow-shapes

the two of you knit together,
how the line of your neck and throat
vanishes into the sweep of your hair
shawling the small bald crown of her head
that's pressed against
one full breast. Your hands
catch light, moulding the globe of shadow
her head composes, steadying
that wool-bundled body
to your flesh. Wherever I look
in that world of light and shade,
the two of you are touching
one another, leaving me
feeling exiled, not unhappy.
And she's asleep, and I'm asleep,
when you stretch
your warm length again beside me.

When the sun glares in the window
and I leave our bed, the baby
is lying beside you,
a half smile on the lips
round your nipple: her eyes
are closed, your eyes
are closed, your head lightly resting
on top of hers. Downstairs,
geraniums and pink impatiens
press flushed winter faces
to the dining-room window,
and everywhere circles
are slowly spinning
in circles, shadows dancing
through rings and widening rings
of light.

Endangered Species

Out the living-room window
I see the two older children burning
household trash under the ash tree
in wind and rain. They move
in slow motion about the flames,
heads bowed in concentration
as they feed each fresh piece in, hair
blown wild across their faces, the fire
wavering in tongues before them
so they seem creatures
half flame, half flesh,
wholly separate from me. All of a sudden

the baby breaks slowly down
through the flexed branches of the ash
in a blaze of blood and green leaves,
an amniotic drench, a gleaming liver-purple
slop of ripe placenta, head first
and wailing to be amongst us. Boy and girl
look up in silence and hold gravely out
flamefeathered arms to catch her,
who lands on her back in their linked
and ashen hands. Later,
when I take her in my arms

for a walk to that turn on the high road
where the sea always startles, I can see
how at intervals she's thunderstruck
by a scalloped green leaf, a shivering
jig of grassheads, or that speckled bee
that pushes itself among
the purple and scarlet parts
of a fuchsia bell. And her eyes are on fire.

Walk, Night Falling, Memory of My Father

Downhill into town
between the flaring azaleas
of neighbour gardens: a cairn of fresh-cut logs
gives off a glow
of broken but transfigured flesh.

My father, meeting me years ago
off a train at Kingsbridge: greenish
tweed cap, tan gaberdine, leaning
on a rolled umbrella, the sun
in his eyes, the brown planes of his face
in shadow, and all of a sudden
old. The distance between us
closes to an awkward, stumbling,
short embrace. Little left

but bits and pieces: pints in Healy's
before tea; a drive with visitors
to Sally Gap; my daughter making
game with his glasses; the transatlantic calls
for an anniversary, birthday,
or to the hospital
before his operations. Moments
during those last days
in the ward, under the big window
where the clouds over the golf course
would break or darken: his unexpected
rise to high spirits, my hand
helping his hand
hold the glass of water. And one memory
he kept coming back to,
of being a child in a white frock,
watching his mother and another woman
in long white dresses and broad straw hats

recline in a rowing-boat on the Boyne
near Navan: how the boat rocked
side to side, the women smiling and
talking in low voices, and him
sitting by himself on the bank
in a pool of sunshine, his little feet
barely reaching the cool water. I remember
how the nurses swaddled his
thin legs in elastic bandages, keeping him
together for a day or two.

Uphill again, the dark now down
and the night voices
at their prayers and panicky conjurations,
one thrush still bravely
shaping in song
the air around him. Fireflies
wink on and off
in lovers' Morse, my own head
floating among them, seeing—
as each opens its heart in silence
and in silence closes—
just how large the dark is. Now,
cold moonglow casts
across this shaking summer world
a thin translucent skin
of snow; tall tree shapes
thicken, whispering; and on ghostly wings
white moths brush by. Indoors again,
I watch them—fallen angels
the size and shade of communion wafers—
beat dusted wings against the screen,
flinging themselves
at this impossible light.

Kitchen Vision

Here in the kitchen, making breakfast,
I find my own view of things
come to light at last: I loom, huge
freckled hands, in the electric kettle's
aluminum belly. In there

the limegreen fridge, military files
of spice jars, and that transfigured window
where the sun breaks flagrant in,
must all recede, draw off, and join
the tiny mourning face
of Botticelli's Venus, hung
above a Lilliputian door. In there

all our household effects
are strictly diminished, pared down
to brilliant miniatures
of themselves—the daily
ineluctable clutter of our lives
contained, clarified, fixed in place
and luminous in ordinary light,
as if seen once and for all
by Jan Steen or Vermeer. And off

in the silver distance the baby
stares at me from her high chair
of a minute's silence,
and you—a mile away at the stove
turning the eggs—turn round

to look at me gazing
at my own
sharply seen misshapen self
in the kettle
that's just starting to sing,
its hot breath steaming.

Cows

They lay great heads on the green bank
and gently nudge the barbed wire aside
to get at the sweet untrodden grass, ears
at an angle flicking and swivelling. Something
Roman in the curled brow, massive
bony scaffolding of the forehead,
the patient, wary look that's
concentrated but detached, as if
the limits of being didn't matter
behind such a lumbering surge of things
in the flesh. Yet in their eyes some deep
unspeakable secret grudge—in part
perhaps their perfect knowledge
of the weight of the world
we hold them to. And something Dutch
about that recumbent mass, their couchant
hefty press of rumination, the solid globe
folded round the ribs' curved hull, barrelling
that enormous belly. The close
rich cud-smell where they stood
grinding down grass to milk
to mother us all; or the childhood stink of stalls,
all milk and piss and dungy straw: what
that umbered word, *cowshed*, conjures.

I remember an Indian file of cows in mist
moving along the lake's lapped margin,
a black and white frieze against the green hill
that leaned over them: the sound
of their cloven steps in shallow water
reached me like the beat of a settled music
in the world we share, and they could have been
plodding towards Lascaux or
across broad prairie-seas of green, even

trampling water-edges such as this one—
trudging through the kingdom-come
of sagas and cattle-raids. Heads bent,
they stepped into mist and silence, the pooling
splash of their hooves a steady progress
that seemed to go on forever, forged
for an eternal trek to grass.

I love the way a torn tuft
of grassblades, stringy buttercup and succulent clover
sway-dangles towards a cow's mouth, the mild teeth
taking it in—purple flowers, green stems and yellow petals
lingering on those hinged lips
foamed with spittle. And the slow chewing sound
as transformation starts: the pulping roughness
of it, its calm deliberate solicitude, its own
entranced herbivorous pacific grace,
the carpet-sweeping sound of breath
huffing out of pink nostrils. Their eyelashes
—black, brown, beige, or white as chalk—
have a miniscule precision, and in the pathos
of their diminutive necessity
are the most oddly human thing about them:
involuntary, they open, close, dealing
as our own do
with what inhabits, encumbering,
the seething waves and quick invisible wilderness
of air, showing the one world
we breathe in
and the common ground—unsteady
under the big whimsical hum of weather—
we all walk across
one step at a time, and stand on.

Station

We are saying goodbye
on the platform. In silence
the huge train waits, crowding the station
with aftermath and longing
and all we've never said
to one another. He shoulders
his black dufflebag and shifts
from foot to foot, restless to be off, his eyes
wandering over tinted windows where he'll sit
staring out at the Hudson's platinum dazzle.

I want to tell him he's entering into the light
of the world, but it feels like a long tunnel
as he leaves one home, one parent
for another, and we both
know in our bones it won't ever
be the same again. What is the air at,
heaping between us then
thinning to nothing? Or those slategrey birds
that croon to themselves in an iron angle
and then take flight—inscribing
huge loops of effortless grace
between this station of shade and the shining water?

When our cheeks rest glancing against each other,
I feel mine scratchy with beard and stubble, his
not quite smooth as a girl's, harder, a faint fuzz
starting—those silken beginnings I can see
when the light is right, his next life
in bright first touches. What ails our hearts? Mine
aching in vain for the words
to make sense of our life together; his
fluttering in dread

of my finding the words, feathered syllables
fidgeting in his throat.

In a sudden rush of bodies
and announcements out of the air, he says
he's got to be going. One quick touch
and he's gone. In a minute
the train—ghostly faces behind smoked glass—
groans away on wheels and shackles, a slow glide
I walk beside, waving
at what I can see no longer. Later,
on his own in the city, he'll enter the underground
and cross the river, going home
to his mother's house. And I imagine
that pale face of his
carried along in the dark glass, shining
through shadows that fill the window
and fall away again
before we're even able to name them.

Sea Dog

The sea has scrubbed him clean
as a deal table.
Picked over, plucked hairless,
drawn tight as a drum—
an envelope of tallow
jutting with rib cage, hips,
assorted bones. The once
precise pads of his feet
are buttons of bleached wood
in a ring of stubble. The skull—
bonnetted, gap-toothed, tapering
trimly to a caul of wrinkles—
wears an air
faintly human, almost ancestral.

Now the tide falls back
in whispers, leaving the two of us
alone a moment together. Trying
to take in what I see, I see
the lye-bright parchment skin
scabbed black by a rack of flies
that rise up, a humming chorus,
at my approach, settle again
when I stop to stare. These
must be the finishing touch, I think,
till I see round the naked neckbone
a tightly knotted
twist of rope, a frayed noose
that hung him up or held him under
till the snapping and jerking stopped.
Such a neat knot: someone
knelt safely down to do it,
pushing those soft ears back
with familiar fingers. The drag end

now a seaweed tangle around legs
stretched against their last leash.

And nothing more
to this sad sack
of bones, these poor enduring remains
in their own body bag. Nothing more.
Death's head here
holds its own peace
beyond the racket-world of feel and fragrance
where the live dog bent, throbbing
with habit, and the quick children
now shriek by on sand—staring,
averting. I go in over my head

in stillness, and see
behind the body and the barefoot children
how on the bent horizon to the west
a sudden flowering shaft of sunlight
picks out four pale haycocks
saddled in sackcloth
and makes of them a flared quartet
of gospel horses—rearing up,
heading for us.

Rights

He has every right to name her.

The nimble muse of History
is what the poet said, rolling his Russian
consonants and vowels around at us like
gravel, *gravitas*, like gravity, the solid
slow motion towards the core. She's

been to bed with him, both of them
out in the cold and tonguetied, but oh
the oily motions of her quickened limbs
there in the dark, nothing between them
but, thin as air, the knifeblade and
—thinner than that—the flash of it
where their blind hips touch,
knowing one another for what they are.

He has earned her name, living at home
for years with her like that, her bruised
lips on his, his eyes wide open
to every wrinkle, nick, and imperfection
of age in her, the blackened orbs
of eyelids, her cracked hands. She's
never the same as he remembers her:

a voice from childhood or a flicker
of cobbled light off water; the door
knocked open at two in the morning
or a letter from a friend in exile; silence
on the very edge of revelation. Or else
the raw igniting ice then fire of vodka
tongued and swallowed; the heartfelt
smell of morning—fresh bread, blue spruce,

snow in May—all the feints, glides and
fancy handwork of that muse of his,

who is nimble as a dancer at the court
of amazement, her beautiful bleeding feet
barely tipping the double blade
she bows and balances and spins on.

Compass Reading

This morning the cat pawed up
against the glass storm-door, her eyes
wild and satisfied, a quiver
of pale grey-brown feathers
between her jaws. Shouting,
slamming open the door, I rescued
the broken neck, closed eyes, tuft
and ruffled wings—the breast
still soft and warm—and placed them
out of harm's way, as if it mattered,
in the mailbox. Later,
under cover of the dark,
I took and threw the titmouse
among the leaves still clinging to trees and hedges
at the back of the house: flying
from my hand it gave, I thought,
the smallest sigh, the way
it broke the air, the air
opening for it, taking its little weight
for the last time, before it fell
with a faint, desiccated splash
among twigs and leaves
where it will lie, grow less itself, unravel
back to bone, to mould, to dust,
to next year's fierce leaf
whose feathers and fine airs
will stand up to anything. I imagine
its first arrested screech, the cat
tasting a salt smear of blood
across tongue and teeth: she knows
the ripe smell of death, the face
of terror, the terminal spasm.
These days I seem as heartless as a lock
that is all innards and bitter tongue:

wherever my ears go, they hear
nothing but clocks ticking, each tick
a distinct penetration of air, a pulsebeat
greeting its own goodbye. And I can see
in the shortlived gauze of dew on the steps
the neat dark footpads of the cat,
who will—for all her satisfactions—
not be appeased.

Diagnosis

To be touched like that
from so far, collusion
of skin and sunlight—one
ray, one cell, the collapse
of fenceworks: I feel mined,
nicked like a leaf
to a brown spot of burn
that catches the eye. Visited.

With one eye open
I probe the small swelling,
hoping to know
this intimate enemy
that bites through bone
if left to its own
staggering devices: so this—
as if a myth had fallen
into the back garden
and stood in my light
when I took out the trash—
is it: detached
and absolute, the word
comes over the phone
and day chills a little, ghosted,
goes briefly out of focus. Somewhere
a knife is sharpening,
my skin shivers: I can see
my own skin as if
it were another—a dear
companion, lover, brother—
shivering. *Malignant.*

Outside, I swim
through a hot storm

of light: head down,
I hurry from shadow
to shadow, eyes on the ground
where I see the fresh tar
sealing the driveway
is cracked open already
with little craters, irresistible
dandelion and crabgrass
knuckling up. Nothing can stop
their coming to a green point,
this hungry thrust
towards light. Here are seeds

songbirds will forage
as the weather hardens
before snow, green wounds
gleaming in tar, life itself
swallowing sunlight. The blacktop
glares at a clear blue sky
and in my eyes the sun
spins a dance of scalpels—
till I pray for cloud, for night's
benign and cooling
graces, to be at ease again
in the friendly
realm of shadows.

Moving

She is moving
out over thresholds
of worn brass,
under scratched lintels.

The rain stops, leaving
the slaphappy song
of full gutters, hornbeam
and hickory leaves

slick with light. She's years
breathing and sleepwalking
among them, putting meals
on the shaky table, making

beds and other decisions.
Standing in the doorway
she drinks the sky in, drowning
under a rush of lilacs

but keeping one eye
on the baby, whose hair
floats in its own silken haze.
At noon she hides herself

in shadows that travel
a sheet of unbleached cotton
hung between two branches,
swaying in sunlight. She's

putting it all behind her,
wondering what shape

forgiveness takes, what name
her father wore

in his suit of bamboo green,
twirling his whiskers
for the ladies and
crooning ragtime, crooning

Schubert. Her mother's face
buries itself in the dust
behind the furniture, turning away,
saying, *I told you so.*

In the cellar,
her husband the woodchuck
mopes among the spent
motors, rooting around

for her tongue. Nothing here
is home anymore—
from gilded doorknobs
and glinting windows

to timber
groaning at the heart
of plaster walls—
so she's moving out

into sea light that seems
to run on and on, knowing
when she's gone
the ghosts will gather

near the fireplace
like the smell of pine resin,

a faint perturbation
shaking the air. She knows

they'll talk together
in low, slow, fathoming voices,
like elders, and then
—when time is ripe—

set out to find her.

Towards Dusk the Porcupine

Startled to see me
where he shuffles onto
the dirt road between stands of trees,

he leans first into the ferns
and clumps of poison ivy
but then comes on, crossing, and I wait

while he levers his spiked amble
to the woods
on the other side

and into the depths of
his domain of moss and bark,
flickering shades, rocks

bright-scabbed with lichen. It's
nearly dusk, but I can see
his body's chalky beige,

the black and white quills
pulsing, the blunt
pig's head tucked low,

the targe of his arse
black as charcoal. On oddly
meditative steps, wavering a little,

he seems aware of bearing
his own body with him
as he enters a crackle of twigs

and dead leaves, doing this
undulant slow waddle—fat Caliban—
into silence and the brown

living kingdom of shade,
his nodding small head
peering shortsighted

at the ground he's covering
hunched over—like Lowell reading.
Suddenly, he stops

to stare glumly back at me,
one brilliant quill of curiosity
taking in

this small walking tree to which
he nods once a bobbing head and then
goes deeper in, to be lost

among last shadows, forgetting me
already, his faint chalky outline
ghosting behind a slim white birch

into invisibility—knowing exactly
what he is, and where, and how
he ends at pointed edges like that

and can cast them off
when needs be, his heart
in its reed basket

a full thumping, the twenty
species of beetle and seed
sweetening his belly.

Breaking Points

for Joe Butwin

They'll all break at some point,
if you can only find it, he says, hoisting
the wedgeheaded heavy axe and coming down with it
in one swift glittering arc: a single *chunnk,*
then the gleam of two half moons of maple
rolling over in the driveway. He finds
his proper rhythm, my strong friend from the west,
standing each half straight up,
then levelling swinging striking
dead centre: two quarters
fall apart from one another
and lie, off-white flesh shining,
on the cracked tarmac. I stand back
and watch him bend and bring to the chopping-place
a solid sawn-off wheel of the maple bough
the unexpected early snow brought down
in a clamorous rush of stricken leafage, a great weight
he walks gingerly under
and gently settles. When he tests it with his eye

I remember a builder of drystone walls
saying the same thing about rocks and big stones,
turning one over and over, hunting its line
of least resistance, then offering it a little
dull tap with his mallet: the stone, as if he'd
slipped the knot holding it together, opened
—cloned—and showed its bright unpolished
inner life to the world. Joe goes on logging
flat-out for an hour, laying around him
the split quarters, littering the tar-black driveway
with their matte vanilla glitter. Seeing
him lean on the axe-shaft

for a minute's headbent silence
in the thick of his handiwork,

I remember standing silent at the centre
of the living-room I was leaving for the last time
after ten years of marriage, the polished pine floor
scattered with the bits and pieces
I was in the aftermath taking with me,
the last battle still singing
in my head, the crossed limbs of the children
sofa-sprawled in sleep. And as soon
as he finishes and comes in, steam
sprouting from his red wet neck
and matted hair, dark maps of sweat
staining his navyblue T-shirt, I want to say
as he drains his second glass of lemonade

that this is the way it is
in the world we make and break
for ourselves: first the long green growing, then
the storm, the heavy axe, those shining remnants
that'll season for a year
before the fire gets them; this is the way
we flail our way to freedom of a sort,
and after the heat and blistering deed of it
how the heart beats in its birdcage of bone
and you're alone
with your own staggered body, its toll
taken, on the nervous verge of
exaltation. But I say nothing, just pour
more lemonade, open a beer, listen

to the tale he tells
of breakage back home—the rending-place
we reach when the labouring heart

fails us and we say
What now? What else? What?
                              And now
in the dusk assembling outside the window
I can see the big gouged maple
radiant where the bough stormed off,
and the split logs
scattered and bright over the driveway—in what
from this Babylonian distance looks like
a pattern of solid purposes or the end of joy.

The Cave Painters

Holding only a handful of rushlight
they pressed deeper into the dark, at a crouch
until the great rock chamber
flowered around them and they stood
in an enormous womb of
flickering light and darklight, a place
to make a start. Raised hands cast flapping shadows
over the sleeker shapes of radiance.

They've left the world of weather and panic
behind them and gone on in, drawing the dark
in their wake, pushing as one pulse
to the core of stone. The pigments mixed in big shells
are crushed ore, petals and pollens, berries
and the binding juices oozed
out of chosen barks. The beasts

begin to take shape from hands and feather-tufts
(soaked in ochre, manganese, madder, mallow white)
stroking the live rock, letting slopes and contours
mould those forms from chance, coaxing
rigid dips and folds and bulges
to lend themselves to necks, bellies, swelling haunches,
a forehead or a twist of horn, tails and manes
curling to a crazy gallop.

Intent and human, they attach
the mineral, vegetable, animal
realms to themselves, inscribing
the one unbroken line
everything depends on, from that
impenetrable centre
to the outer intangibles of light and air, even
the speed of the horse, the bison's fear, the arc

of gentleness that this big-bellied cow
arches over its spindling calf, or the lancing
dance of death that
bristles out of the buck's
struck flank. On this one line they leave
a beak-headed human figure of sticks
and one small, chalky, human hand.

We'll never know if they worked in silence
like people praying—the way our monks
illuminated their own dark ages
in cross-hatched rocky cloisters,
where they contrived a binding
labyrinth of lit affinities
to spell out in nature's lace and fable
their mindful, blinding sixth sense
of a god of shadows—or whether (like birds
tracing their great bloodlines over the globe)
they kept a constant gossip up
of praise, encouragement, complaint.

It doesn't matter: we know
they went with guttering rushlight
into the dark; came to terms
with the given world; must have had
—as their hands moved steadily
by spiderlight—one desire
we'd recognise: they would—before going on
beyond this border zone, this nowhere
that is now here—leave something
upright and bright behind them in the dark.

Woman at Lit Window

Perhaps if she stood for an hour like that
and I could stand to stand in the dark
just looking, I might get it right, every
fine line in place: the veins of the hand
reaching up to the blind-cord, etch
of the neck in profile, the white
and violet shell of the ear
in its whorl of light, that neatly
circled strain against a black
cotton sweater. For a few seconds

she is staring through me
where I stand wondering what I'll do
if she starts on that stage of light
taking her clothes off. But she only
frowns out at nothing or herself
in the glass, and I think I could,
if we stood for an hour like this,
get some of the real details down. But
already, even as she lowers the blind,
she's turning away, leaving a blank

ivory square of brightness
to float alone in the dark, the faint
grey outline of the house
around it. Newly risen, a half moon
casts my shadow on the path
glazed with grainy radiance
as I make my slow way back

to my own place
among the trees, a host of fireflies
in fragrant silence and native ease
pricking the dark around me
with their pulse, ungovernable, of light.

Breakfast Room

1.

The words have always stirred a sudden
surge of light, an air of new beginnings, something
neat and simple, a space
both elemental and domestic—because, perhaps,
they bear a sort of innocent sheen
of privilege, a room so set apart
for an event so ordinary, a glimmer of ritual
where mostly we know only broken facts, bits and pieces
stumbling numbly into one another. Here
is a murmur of voices, discretion's homely music
of spoons on saucers, the decent movements
people make around each other—eager
to let themselves become themselves again
after the night's uncertain journeys. Or it may be
the secret knowing smiles that lovers save, sitting
to face one another in their quaint conspiracy
of hope and saying, *Pass the milk, please,* but meaning
Nothing has ever pleased me more
than how your naked shoulders and the small of your back
lay on my spread hands; your earlobe, tongue, wide eyes
entering half-frightened mine in the dark.

2.

And in Bonnard's *The Breakfast Room,* you'll see
the impeccable ordinary order he finds in things:
white, slateblue, the tablecloth bears its own still life
of teapot, cream pitcher, sugarbowl,
china cup and scalloped saucer, the half glass of raspberry juice,
bread in yellow napkins, that heaped dish
of purple figs and a peach. And, as if
accidental by the French windows—

through which morning light
passes its binding declarative sentence
on every detail—a woman stands
almost out of the picture, her back
against the patterned drapes, dressed to go out
and giving a last look back, her eyes and strict lips
asking directly, *You think this
changes anything?* Yet she too
is part of this stillness, this sense
that things are about to achieve
illumination. Beyond the window
a stone balustrade, and beyond that
nature's bluegreen tangle tangles
with the light that's melting one thing
into another—blue, scrubbed green, strawgold,
a house with a white and lilac roof
at the end of a sunstreaked avenue
on which the summer trees are
blobs of turquoise. Inside, quite distinct,
that woman is held to her last look back,
her sudden pulsebeat shaking
all the orderly arrangements
of the table. Through its
ambivalence of light, its double tongue
of detail and the world at large,
we are brought into the picture, into a kingdom
we might find under our noses: morning's
nourishment and necessary peace; a pause
on the brink of something always
edging into shape, about to happen.

That Ocean

To love the scrubbed exactitudes
and the dimmer thing
that shivers at the brink.

There is, for example, the intimate rustle
of this woman's loose skirt, rayon,
as she hurries up a flight of stone steps
ahead of me: I slow down to relish
the faintly kissing sound of threads,
threads and flesh.

Or under a quilted bundling-up of cloud,
a crow's broad black wing
palping air: dark assemblage
of force and voice and appetite and air,
a poise, a buoyancy, a beating
of bone light as breath, burning with purpose.

I despair of dealing sincerely
with the crow, the brushings of desire,
that woman's headlong motion, the black farewell,
steady caresses opening the air,
inflamed soliloquy of the skirt,
fragrant dialogue of flesh and texture.

Under this abrasive rain
the grass, dead all winter,
glows like straw-spun fabled gold,
and two kinds of willow
—the local and the Babylonian—
flush and swell demented: one
rises in upright ecstasy, the other
overarched with grief. Between them
they occupy the wary air

with embering green, bleached amber,
where—when the rain grows less—
I can hear the little singers
going mad again.

Or there is the absolute intimacy
of eating. To stand in the kitchen
sniffing a bowl of duck fat
is to catch a scent the creature never had
of itself: it is offering up
its essence, the way
neck feathers offered once
an iridescence to the eye one morning,
swivelling in front of you
on a flat dazzle of water. And so
our own essence
is by nature beyond us
and will be rendered after.

At uncommon intervals of attention
we remember ourselves
at one with the world: we enter
the network, a thicket of stillness
where in early spring a sapling of apple or cherry
sends out where it stands
inside the wire fence containing the graveyard
spray after spray of blossom
to stagger the eye
at the stolid grey threshold
of gravestones scoured by rain. And this

may be, you imagine, what
in the dream of good government
Lorenzetti's Peace is dreaming
where she lounges
relaxed, empty, ready for anything

—for the end of art, is it,
or simply listening in
to what might happen, the grasp
of dancers in a ring, their linked hands
a finished circle? Through it all, all
this seething, I walk
beneath a black umbrella,
behind a bright bead-curtain of rain.

What Remains

Silken limegreen wings of two luna moths
pulsing gently on the shadowed screen door
all morning. A stretch of thigh
bared in sunlight—silksmooth and tanned
between sandalwood and dry sherry. A faint
scarlet fleck along one cheekbone, white
twist of silk scarfing the throat. Mooncurve
of a brick-pink fingernail; tonguetip
vanishing behind a gleam of teeth or
travelling—all fleshed texture and blood-heat—
the nicked lip, making it glisten. A black smudge
thickening a single eyelash, and under a light
rose-checkered dress the long outline
of a leg, a solid shadow. One hand splayed
on the breathing rise and fall of a brown belly:
white starfish on a rock, or a stencilled hand
come to light on a cave wall
where torches reel and leap
across the dark. Or else it is
a calf-length skirt of early mist, a blouse
birchleaf green, one goldspiked
lavender glitter of garnets, a sandal's
spiralling leather strap, jangling brass anklets,
or the sudden juddering ripple of a hip
as the breath stops and then
comes back again in time. Such abandoned
bits and pieces as my eyes pick over
and that quicken in me, rising
to mind as whole bodies once more,
and all their covered, incandescent bones.

Two Gathering

for Kate

After supper, the sun sinking fast, Kate and I
have come to the shore at Derryinver
to gather mussels. Across cropped grass, rocks,
we walk to the water's edge where low tide
has exposed a cobbling of cobalt blue shells, others
tucked in clusters under a slick fringe
of seaweed. In my wellingtons
I enter shallow water, bending over
and wresting from their native perch
the muddy clumps of molluscs, rinsing them
in salt water that clouds and quickly clears again
as the tide laps, a slow cat, against me, then
pushing my handfuls into the white plastic bag
I've laid out of the water's way on seaweed.
Kate, in sneakers, is gathering hers
off dry rocks behind me: almost sixteen,
her slim form blossoms in jeans
and a black T-shirt, long hair falling over
as she bends, tugs, straightens
with brimming hands, leans like a dancer
to her white bag, looks out to me and calls
So many! Have you ever seen so many! her voice
a sudden surprise in that wide silence
we stand in, rejoicing—as she always does
and now I must—at the breathless plenitude
of the world, this wondrous abundance
offering itself up to us as if we were
masters of the garden, parts of the plenary
sphere and circle, our bodies belonging
to the earth, the air, the water, fellow creatures
to the secret creatures we gather
and will tomorrow kill for our dinner.

When I bend again—my hands pale groping starfish
under water—it is Kate's own life I fumble for,
from the crickets singing her name
the September afternoon she was born
to the balance she strikes
between separated parents, her passion
for maths, the names of her lost boys,
or the way she takes my arm
when we take a walk on Wing Road
or up the hill from Tully to the cottage. This instant
I can feel her eyes on my bent back, seeing me
standing over my ankles in water, the slow tide
climbing my boots, my cautious
inelastic stepping between elements
when I place the mussels I've gathered
in the bag. And if I turn to look,
I'll see a young woman rising out of sea-rocks, bearing
the salmon and silver air on her shoulders,
her two hands spilling a darkblue arc, about
to take a dancer's step: I hear the muffled clack
of live shells filling her bag.

In our common silence we stay
aware of one another, working together,
until she calls out—*Have you seen*
their colours? Brown and olive and bright green
and black. I thought they were only navy blue—
delighted by variety, the minute ripple of things
under water or changing in air, the quick patterns,
as if the world were one intricate vast equation
and she relished picking it over, seeing the figures
unfold and in a split surprising second
edge out of muddle into elegant sense, the way
she's explained to me her love of maths
as a journey through multiple views to a moment
of—she said it—'vision', you simply see it

all in place before your eyes: a flowering branch
of impeccable sense, number and grace
shimmering in a single figure, a shard of truth
shining like the head of a new nail
you've just, with one stroke, driven home.

Feeling the drag and push of water, I know it's time
to move and I do, inching backwards, my hands
still scrabbling under rubbery weed-fronds
for the mussels' oval stony bulk, their brief
umbilical resistance as I twist them
from their rock, swirl in water, add them
with drippling chill hands to the bag, sensing
the summer dusk falling all over us. *Dad look! A heron!*
standing not twenty yards from us
on the hem of the tide: a grey stillness
staring at nothing
then flicking his serpent-neck and beak
into the water and out, taking a single deliberate step
and then on slow opening wings
rising and flap-gliding across the inlet, inland, heavy
and graceful on the air, his legs
like bright afterthoughts dangling. *He's so big,*
she calls, *How does he do it?* and across
the raw distance of rock and water I call back,
It's the span of his wings, he uses the air,
thinking about question and answer, the ways
we're responsible to one another, how
we use our airy words to lift us up
above the dragging elements we live in
towards an understanding eloquent and silent
as blood is or the allergies I've handed
to her system—our bodies' common repugnance
to penicillin, sulfa—all the buried codes
that bind us in a knot even time
cannot untangle, diminishing, in a way,

the distance between us. *Did you see,* I hear my voice,
his legs? The way they dangled? Thin—
her voice comes back to me—*as sticks,*
and the colour of pearl. Funny
how he tucked them in, putting them away,
and she drops a castanet handful
of mussels into her bag.
                                        My hands
are blueish, a small breeze riffles water,
the spur of land we're on
is drowned in shade: we've gathered enough
and it's time to go. She watches me wading
through bright, light-saving pools, reaches
a helping hand when I clamber up rock
above the seaweed line where she stands waiting
on grass the sheep have bitten to a scut,
their tidy shit-piles of black pellets
scattered all over. With pleasure we behold
the two bulging bags I've draped
in glistering layers of olivebrown bladderwrack,
both of us thinking of the dinner we'll have
tomorrow: brown bread, white wine, a green
salad, the steaming heaps of open shellfish
—ribboned in onion, carbuncled
with chunks of garlic—the plump dull-orange
crescent of each one gleaming
in its mottled shell, sea-fragrance curling off
the greybright salty peppered soup
they've offered up to us, and in it the brilliance
of lemon wedges swimming. At least once each summer
we have a family feast like this, and I picture
her delight in dipping buttered bread, laying
a hot mussel on her tongue, the squirt of sea-tang and flesh
against her teeth, sipping the wine that's still
a stranger to her palate, remembering
the way the sun went down behind the two of us

as we gathered dinner, as if our lives
were always together and this simple.
                                    Now
we stand side by side for a minute or two
in silence, taking the small bay in and the great shade
spreading over sea and land: across the water,
on a sloping headland of green fields, we see
how a stopped hand of sunlight still
in the middle distance lingers, brightening
one brief patch of ground with uncanny light
so I cannot tell if I'm looking at a moment past
of perfect knowledge, or a bright future
throbbing with promise. Then Kate
is giving me, again, her words: *I wonder*
will it strike us over here, is what
I hear her say—her words, unanswered,
hanging between us as we turn to go.

FOUR

Statue

This boy is on the verge of walking
past me, about to go where I can't imagine
his whole body at one with itself
from the lips' full smile to the small
seed-bearing pouch between his thighs,
the muscled legs steady, ready to step
through any drawback or impediment
—even death itself, its wall of glass—
and not turn a curl amongst the bunched
unshockable waves of his hair: he is
a summary of boys, no one in particular,
the tight flesh at apogee, archaic
but recognizable (for all the remote beauty
of his nakedness, his vacant eyes)
as anyone's son on the cusp of manhood,
who will draw himself to his full height
and, holding both those wary hands
loose by his sides, consider in silence
the life that's brought him precisely to this
point of being born again, walking away.

Night Figure

She hovers over the ache of thresholds: that brass
doorknob and the cream paint chipped at the jamb
enter her face again, so close she doesn't notice.

She needs to hear us breathing, the three of us
pitching into sleep in the one room, tucked in
by a faint smell of face powder, sticky touch of lips.

Snare-beat of rain on the roof, the rain spitting
against the window. *It's spilling rain,*
she'll say to herself, *he'll be drowned out in it.*

As if underwater, she stands listening
to the house and all its stunned tongues
gather round her heart. Rumours of being

rush into the instant: a bus coughs by
on Clareville Road, quick steps
syncopate through rain, a bicycle bell

jings in the dark; *squeek squeek* of pedals
against wind and hill. When she moves
into their front bedroom, she sees

from the window a hurrying figure, hears
the little brickish *clik* that high heels
make on stone. A deep pain starts

to open her heart, and she's the secret
goings-on in hives—a slow gathering
and translation, the finished, overflowing

golden comb. Nothing now, *nothing*—
till his key comes fumbling the hall-door,
the sudden rush of air

as the door shuffles open, raw
against the hall's linoleum. A hint of stagger
in the hallway; heavy sit in the muffled chair;

his lidded eyes haze over, blinking: two hearts
heaving like mad. Behind closed doors
the air listens to a huffle of voices. She can feel,

when the petals of pain and rage
have closed again, her vacant relief: the house
complete at last: she can sleep. So

she lies beside his breath, her eyes open
and our house a hive of silence
round her head, her splitting head. Fingernails of rain

are tapping for help against the window: *Let us in,*
let us in, can't you? Then thickened silence
levels the dark, taking the bed

she lies on, and she slides—nothing stops her—
into the wooden dusk
of wardrobes, down the sheer drop of sleep.

Women Going

You know the ordinary ways they go
from you and from the stark daylight
staring through an open door. This girl
leans her lips to the beak of a dove
she holds against her heart as if
insinuating the best way out and back
and whispering, *Now I have to go.*

On a stone doorpost the young wife
arches her stopped body, one hand
flat across her belly, the other
raised to straighten the seamless veil
through which the full moons of her earrings
just appear, signalling a change of state
and no way back to the here and now
of things, to the honeysuckle open air
she's been breathing. The lady of the house

holds up one necklace after another
chosen from the jewelbox a servant offers
and eyes the way it might belong
between the jut of her neckbone
and where her breasts begin, fitting her
for the road that opens ahead now
and night falling: *This one,* she says
at last, picking the pearls with a clasp
curved like a wishbone. And now

across the busy street you see a man
lean into the back of a taxi
where a woman's face is barely visible
looking back into his and not flinching
as they dispossess each other into absence,
and the door in that black cloud closes over

whatever it is they say above the roar
of rush-hour traffic. He bends away,

and you know when he looks again
she'll be gone, and in her place will be
this absence beating its stone wings
over every ordinary corner of the day
she's left, and left him in.

Bat

With no warning
and only the slightest
whisshing sound
it was in the room with me,
trapped and flashing
wall to wall. Flat
black leather wings
that never stop, body
become a baby fist,
tiny head
blindly peering,
a wild heart
out of its element.

Between its teeth
it needles a piercing
inaudible pulse-scream
that sets its course
and keeps it beating,
barely grazing
walls, wardrobe,
chest of drawers, all
—pitch pine, walnut,
Irish oak—smelling
of outdoors, I suppose,
and sending it
round the bend
while I
try to follow its
dodgy swerves, duck
when it flutters at me,
fumble after
with my eyes.

This all happens
in a fathomless
daylight silence
which binds us
for a hypnotised
little while,
making me feel
as the creature
circles and circles
that I've been kissed
repeatedly
in sleep, light lips
brushing, gone.

At last—by luck
as much as
navigation—it flits
through the window
I've scrambled open,
leaving me
to track its zigzags
over bright grass,
by light afflicted,
desperate
for the dark. Now,

months later,
I still remember
how it tackled exactly
its woeful task,
a heartbeat holding it
to scents and glimmers
of bloodsap, wingwhisper,
nightsqueaks, void,
the sheer (to my ear)
stoic silence

of the whole operation
showing rightly
the likes of us
how to behave
in a tight corner:

Keep quiet
keep moving
try everything
more than once
steer
by glancing touches
aftershocks
the fleeting grace
of dark advances
quick retreats
till you find
in your way
with no warning
the window
open.

Couple

1.

He is hearing out the crickets.
She leans back in a chair

so the light, creaking,
can find her eyes. She stays like that,

braced and at rest, eyes closed,
eyelids warm. On the porch of salt

he stands in shadow, feeling
the season fly down his throat.

His heart will burst. All he can say
is the leaves are turning.

2.

They'll have dinner together.
The little tongue of flame

will sing in the wineglass, the butter
be a glitter of liquid gold

running away
through pale green

asparagus fingers. The fleshed
wedge of swordfish

swimming in cream; a tiny
white dome of rice

on flowered plates. It will all
be there for a moment:

their murmuring talk, the child
asleep upstairs, their dim

reflections in the dark
uncurtained window, glinting

and leaning into each other
with forks suspended. The image

of lips moving in silence,
and that one tongue of fire

pulsing. The full
particular

livid taste in their heart.

Outing

Granted the Atlantic between us, I can only imagine
walking in on you asleep in an armchair
the nurses have pillowed, your white-haired head
and the powdery skin of your face tilted sideways,
your chin sinking into the sag of your breast
where one button in the pale blue frock's undone.

When you fell down that Sunday last summer
and your poor shoulder buckled under you,
I could tell—trying to lift that terrible weight
from the lavatory's slippery stone floor—
the way things were. Still, as every other summer,
you loved our drives out of Bloomfield
to the sea, loved sitting in the car up Vico Road,
staring off over water towards Howth or Bray,
Greystones, the Sugarloaf (as plain on a good day,
you'd say, as your hand). And no matter
even if it rained, it was always a cleansing
breath of fresh air for you, a sort of tranquil
hovering above things, the known world
close enough to touch: blackberry bushes
and high-gabled houses; foxglove and bracken;
the hundred steep steps down to the sea.
I used to wonder if it ever crossed your mind
that the next life you firmly believed in
might be something like that—the same peace
of simply sitting, looking at whatever was there
and passing: older couples with their dogs,
salted children streeling from the sea,
a parish priest swinging his black umbrella,
the occasional brace of lovers in step. Over
the lowered window you'd smile
your genteel *Good afternoon!* to them all,
and seem for this little while at least

almost out of reach of your old age—its slumped
and buzzing vacancies, blank panic, garbled talk.

But now, near another summer, they tell me
your temperature flares, falls, flares again,
and nothing to be done. Alive, they say,
but in ways not there at all, you've left us
and gone on somewhere, and I remember
how as kids we trailed your solid figure
when you pushed the youngest in his pram
and turned to call us all to catch up, *Hold on
to the pram now, don't let go*. I remember
the pounding silence when you'd hide
and all of a sudden come dashing out
behind your voice—your arms like wings,
laughing our names to the air around us,
the sound of your glad breath bearing down.
But when I appear in a week or so, I'm told
you won't know me, the way you mostly
don't know the others, and I remember
your phrase when I'd come home at last
after months at school: *I wouldn't know you*,
you'd say, holding me away at arm's length
or in a hug, *I just wouldn't know you*,
only this time the same delighted words
will die in your mouth, and you'll be
two puzzled milk-pale hazel eyes
staring at this bearded stranger. You've left
already, knowing well what I've no words for:
the smudge and shaken blur of things, bodies
floating by like clouds, brittle sunshine
flapping through a window to your lap,
days in their nameless, muffled procession
or the frank night-scurry of dream after dream,
each with its seepage, bat-flash, dear faces.

Here among woods and hills of New Hampshire
it's you I think of when I watch the mountains
appear and disappear in mist, the shape of things
changing by the minute. Were you with me now,
I'd show you these blowsy irises, and those
exploding globes of rhododendron, lady slippers
in the shade, or flagrant and shortlived the blaze
of the yellow day-lilies. You could listen out
for the pure soul music the hermit thrush makes
alone in the echo-chamber of the trees, his song
a blessing, you'd say, to your one good ear.
Side by side, we'd sit in this screened gazebo
facing Mount Monadnock, and you might try
the mountain's name a few times on your tongue,
getting it wrong, wrong again, until
you'd give your helpless laugh, give up, and say
For God's sake don't annoy me, will you,
whatever you call it. Can't I just call it
Killiney, Sugarloaf, or Howth—what matter?
We'd agree on this, *God knows,* and you
would sit back to enjoy the view, the delicious
sense of yourself just sitting—the way
we've always done, we're used to—pleased
for the moment with what we've got,
and pleased at how that big green hill
swims in and out of view as the mist
lifts and settles, and lifts, and settles.

Pause

for Kira

The weird containing stillness of the neighbourhood
just before the school bus brings the neighbourhood kids
home in the middle of the cold afternoon: a moment
of pure waiting, anticipation, before the outbreak of anything,
when everything seems just, seems *justified*, just hanging
in the wings, about to happen, and in your mind you see
the flashing lights flare amber to scarlet, and your daughter
in her blue jacket and white-fringed sapphire hat
step gingerly down and out into our world again
and hurry through silence and snow-grass
as the bus door sighs shut
and her own front door flies open and she finds you
behind it, father-in-waiting, the stillness in bits
and the common world restored as you bend
to touch her, take her hat and coat from the floor
where she's dropped them, hear the live voice of her
filling every crack. In the pause
before all this happens, you know something
about the shape of the life you've chosen to live
between the silence of almost infinite possibility and that
explosion of things as they are—those vast unanswerable
intrusions of love and disaster, or just the casual scatter
of your child's winter clothes on the hall floor.

Journey

Get the word and go.

The river is waking:
the train breaks morning open
over water. Fleets
of sleek sailboats bob at anchor.

Steely sheen. The green of the far shore
splashed with light. White
blouses of women
touching their fragrant patient bodies.

A tall bird bends
to its own shiver-image
in water, refreshing itself
before flight. The river

runs down to salt, and the sun
of the summer solstice
transforms water
to one wide flash of glass.

Mortuary after mortuary
of spent cars, ghosts
of tenement windows
flapping plastic: the city

suddenly lapping my ankles
with soot and clamour,
till the plane pushes up
through clouds, climbing

with streamlined heavy effort
towards the rarer medium:

we're leaving earth
and leaping into the clear

blue dome spread over. Below us,
a firmament of cloud
fashions a soft nest
for sunlight, bulky crests

of almost otherworldly weather,
nothing but radiance and shade
stretching as far
as the eye can see, a picture

of speechless peace, a world
that's not our world
yet we've come into it
as into some kingdom

of tranquillity
where all our tears
will be—as they say—
wiped away, although

this very minute
I might imagine
something still anchored
in her remains, as if

waiting for this face
to bend over her final face,
this firstborn voice to say
the word, any word,

and let her go.

Dublin, June 1990

Whistling in the Dark

1.

The day of her waking and last exposure, I saw
the dark cloud of a tree against the light
and thought of the various ways a body had
of being invisible: all that solid wood and breathing leaf
washed out to an airy presence
in the dismembering energies of light. Later,
unprepared, I would see the breathless, full
provisional rigidity of death, that loved body—lit
by its history—become a lump of wooden absence
wearing a flowered nightie and the ghost of a smile. Just
another way of being invisible: the temple stunned,
cheeks fleshy but cold as stone, hands locked,
and nothing to break the silence between us
but the sound of my escaping breath as it brushed
over the open secret of her *not-here, not-here.*

2.

At dusk near water I watch the waves, the luminous rain,
and a plover scurry over rocks and weed,
whistling to its hunger. Through gathering mist
the foghorn moans, and the rain in my face
turns me towards town again, which is all of a sudden
lit up and glittering, as if there were some pattern to it
after all. The bird prods a small rock, and I hear
the splash and wriggle of something alive under there
and a whistle of excited hunger. Silence. Then the blind cry
of warning off water. The world gets smaller and smaller. Time
to go home and I start, swallowing those two big words as I go.

3.

When I stand with my right hand touching the back
of her crossed hands, I can tell without looking
that the livid veins and that bright traveller, the blood,
have settled for snow at last. Aflame once
in the friendly element of air, heartsfire beating in tongues,
they've fallen asleep in a snowbank, breathing a small hole
into the cold, and sliding in—as a snake in winter
makes a space to sleep and wake in. So, pulling the air
in their wake, these ardent pilgrims have turned
to a world of snow, leaving nothing but a little melt-mark
behind them, shape of a starched white nightdress
where tiny red flowers have all this while been blooming.

4.

Out early in the morning, I see ebony pellets of deer shit
glinting with dew, and on moss filaments a few
first fractures of light. The white of a broken mushroom flashes
like a fish turning at the surface, or could be the gleam
of a piece of steamed plaice laid open before her eyes
delighting in it, the fork dipped then wavering to her mouth,
all lost for one unfrightened instant
in the shriven intimacy of expectation, taste, the moister instincts
ticking over. And I have, across the table, nothing to say,
trying to fix this minute among its poor relations.

What Doesn't Happen

Would you have raised your head and opened your eyes
and astonished us all with a few sentences of recognition
if I'd walked in any time before the end and taken
your light hand in my hand still hot from the journey?
And then died anyway, since there was only one way?
Of course I imagined something dramatic—me freeing you
from sleep, stopping time a while to get our stories settled,
but then I was looking up from the grave we'd laid you in
to see the tree in a heavy overcoat of green and everything
growing away like mad, a sudden blustering thundery rain
to remove all traces. So I speak in a low voice, knowing
I speak to nothing there, nothing coming through to here
where earth is covered in small translucent pods, the air
a congregation of feathered seeds taken by the breeze
and floating to wherever they'll fall and, some, take root.

Yesterday I stood to look at a deer half-hidden in leaves,
a big doe still as a brown statue: her ears cupped up
like dish antennae, her tail a white stain, the whole field
between us as I strained, unable to see her eyes—only
the thick tan stalk of her neck, the head erect and pointed
in my direction, a scab of light on her brow's dead centre
as if something glowed there, the two of us facing across
that wide divide. Wondering would she scare if I went closer,
I started slowly towards her: still she stayed, not a flicker
of fright, just this tuned thing alert without trepidation
and watching me move through the tall grass in her direction
until I stopped, thought better of it, then edged back
to the path, my eyes still fixed on that steady glow
above where her sharper eyes, I felt, were finding mine.

What's to be done with this desperate balance, this pendulum
to which even lovers are strapped in passion and doubt,
clocks ticking and seed-pods clicking off our minutes? There is

no life I can put you back into, Ma—with your lipstick and rings,
your flans, fried cod and floury potatoes, your glass of Paddy
or Bristol Cream, ears eager for the same old stories, eyes
for the photos seen over and over; your rosary beads, seat
in the sun, sweet tooth, love of summer—and I only remember
when we'd be together and I'd have to go, you'd hear
the finished day shut with a click, the door close
on you and on my voice saying, *See you tomorrow,* until
that last time, your little surrendering wave through the window,
no more words. So now there can be no forgetting

your white hair and fallen breasts, the slack, soap-coloured
skin of your belly, slow feet on the stairs, the way your teeth
grew darker, looser, falling out in dismay. But you'd insist
we keep in mind the good times too—those times you'd say
I almost died laughing, or the two of us talking
in the warm kitchen, nothing but steamy diagonals of sunlight
standing between us, your ripe arms bare to the elbow
and the close air heavy with the homely smells
of a chicken growing brown in its own juices, parsnips
mashed with butter and pepper, Sunday pudding. But here
and now, as a sudden storm starts to clear the air—turning
trees heavy, impenetrable, with a novel green light—I know
there's neither going back nor going forward, only this
running in place as usual, trying to see more deeply in.

Heirloom

Among some small objects
I've taken from my mother's house
is this heavy, hand-size, cut-glass saltcellar:
its facets find her at the dining-room table
reaching for the salt or passing it to my father
at the far end, his back to the window.

The table's a timebomb: father hidden
behind the newspaper, mother filling our
plates with food; how they couldn't meet
each other's eyes. When he'd leave early
for an armchair, *Just a glance at the evening paper*,
she'd sit until—all small talk exhausted—

we kids would clear the tea-things away,
stack dirty dishes by the scullery sink,
and store the saltcellar in the press
where it would absorb small tears of air
till the next time we'd need its
necessary, bitter addition. Now it figures

on our kitchen table in Poughkeepsie,
is carried to the diningroom for meals—
its cheap cut glass outlasting flesh and blood
as heirlooms do. I take its salt
to the tip of my tongue, testing its savour,
and spill by chance

a tiny white hieroglyph of grains
which I pinch
in my mother's superstitious fingers
and quick-scatter over my left shoulder,
keeping at bay and safe
the darker shades.

Ghosts

1.

One by one, in a fringe of frayed light,
they'll enter the narrow room
where you lie in the dark—a stone pressed
 between chest and throat, the sting
of salt on your tongue—letting the fragments
reassemble. You'll learn to live
with the curtains drawn, the stammering
smallest breath of them remembered,
and everything you didn't understand
staring back at you
as pure fact, their closed faces.

2.

Sackcloth, the clouds come down as ash.
The scorched word, *Angel,*
drifts up the chimney. Nothing breathes
where the rose window
has lost its magic, dancers wither
into smoke, forlorn gums keep their teeth
agape in a glass of cold water.
And nothing in the dark
but a tuft of beige hair and a wisp of white
whispering at the window, *We have come
this far.* The air
raw as a peeled turnip, a vague
turnip-coloured dawn
daubing the east, the shell of one bell
bringing the snifflers out
to eight o'clock Mass. At the front

window of this widowed house a face—
though you know it isn't there—stares.

3.

I can see the two of them moving
slowly over the sand away from me,
grown very small in the growing distance:
her pale blue cardigan; his olivegreen
tweed jacket; the slow roll of her hips;
his straight back. The light hovers then,

till I see no sign before me, only know
they've entered into a last glimpse
of her hand reaching out for help
over a rocky place, and he stopping
at last and reaching his hand back
for her hand just as I hoped he would
before the sun went in and I have to hurry
from a coming shower. They have

become the barest glimmer, as if passed
through a glass wall in air, walking
on the other side of light. For minutes
I see nothing but rocks, the tide
that rises to cover them, taupe-green and
navy-blue tongues foaming closer. Then,

is that them again? Two tiny figures
float along the far wall of the pier
and are gone, nothing but a shaft of sunlight
clinging a minute to the stone
until it too seems to shiver and enter itself
and go, a luminous late withering, leaving

me to stare at where it was. You take
what you can, even light on stone:
those two hands knowing their own
instant's touch, the exact exchange of that
before the loaded cloud comes over,
slows down light, and shakes it out as rain.

Stone Flight

A piece of broken stone, granular granite, a constellation
of mica through its grey sky, one chalky pink band
splitting slabs of grey, it fits snug enough in the palm
of your hand. Toss it up and it falls, an arc saying *Yes*
to gravity again, and saying in its one dunt of a word
when it falls with a thump on the soft path, *I'm here
to stay*. At a pinch, you might strip things down to this:
compact and heavy the pressure on your hand; the light arc
as if things weighed nothing, casting off; the apogee
and turn, catching a different kind of light; the steady,
at the speed of gravity, descent; and then that dull but
satsifying *thunk* to stop, its cluster of consonantal solids
allowing no air in, no qualifying second thought
as it lands like the one kiss to his scratchy cheek
at greeting or bedtime you'd give your father, or maybe
rolls an inch or two—depending on the chance of grit,
pebbles, the tilt of ground at this precise point
in the wide world, or the angle of itself it falls on. Not,
however, that *grunt* the condemned man makes
some fifty far-fetched seconds or so
after the injection has done our dirty work, the slump
of his head and just once that grunt as the body
realises its full stop, almost surprised. Nor yet the small
grunt of surprised satisfaction you've heard
when you're as deep inside and around one another
as you two can be, body bearing body away and
you push, once, and flesh grunts with a right effort
that seems outside, beyond the two of you, something
old and liberated, a sort of joyous punctuation point
in the ravelling sentence that leaves you both as one
breathless wrap of skin and bone, your double weight
hardly anything as you kiss your way down and back
to your own selves, maybe rolling an inch or two
and then lie still, alive, in matter again, the tick of it

starting to fill the silence. But not that either—just a stone
that leaves your opened hand, lets go of you, ascends
to its proper pitch this once and descending, kissing
gravity every inch, to hit the ground you picked it from
with hardly a thought, and staying there, mica stars
glittering in its granite firmament, a stone among stones
in the dust at a verge of meadowgrass and wild carrot.

Shed

You wouldn't know it had been there at all, ever,
the small woodshed by the side of the garage
that a falling storm-struck bough demolished
some seasons back, the space and remains now
overcome by weeds, chokecherry, wild rose brambles.
But, at the verge of where it stood, a peach tree
I'd never seen a sign of before has pushed
its skinny trunk and sparse-leaved branches up
above that clutter into the thoroughfare of light
and given us, this fall, a small basketful
of sweet fruit the raccoons love too and sit at midnight
savouring, spitting the stones down where the shed
used to stand—those bony seeds ringing along
the metal ghost of the roof, springing into the dark.

Angel Looking Away

Somewhere they are throwing
rice and rose water,
carrying the coffins shoulder-high,

but on Pisano's pulpit the angel
is turned away in sorrow
from the slaughter of the innocents

and in the interrogation centre
a man has turned
away from the polished steel table

on which a man—
calloused tallow soles
stretched towards us—is twitching

as a live wire
wide as its own glitter
kisses the eye of his penis

while another man
is gazing down, perplexed,
at the naked figure on the table

and holding a small black box
with two switches: between
a thumb and tapered index finger

one switch is being gently eased
to the ON position, and now
the poem is looking

at the angel looking away,
at that handsome strong youth
in his marble sorrow,

and you know
it can do nothing
not to lose its tongue.

Headlines

I knock on the tree. It opens
into my mother's grave: a beech tree
coming into leaf. Wan green
springlight: one wind-up wren
clicking for cover, making her bed
in a tenement of dead wood.

The border crawls
along these little hills the ice
let fall: it could almost be invisible
but for just what happens:
one more bedroom mirror in bits
and shivers, the spreading chill.

'Victims,' they say, and 'killers'—
running out of words. The ice
waits for a change of heart. Here
is a girl's head, a man's hand
holding the gun against it: she feels
the small round point of it for a second.

Ordinary days. Spring's slow
explosions all over the place:
beech leaves, maybush, lacy
sprays of laurel, cherry blossom's
pink boudoir. Such a crush
of shameless life, you'd forget everything

except this jeepful of soldiers
patrolling the estate, buttoned-up

and clutching sten-guns. In her last years
my mother never read
beyond the headlines: *It isn't real,*
she'd say, folding the paper and going

back to her window. *How could it be?*

Horses

1.

Although they seldom muscled above me,
I remember being dwarfed always
in the stone fountain of their force,
rawly afraid, awe-struck at something
vast, a violence harnessed and hauling
a cart of scrap metal through our tidy suburb,
men with wild weatherbeaten faces
snapping the reins. The neck's
thick branching grace I remember,
and the fleshed bones in their legs
that I saw from the footpath or, once,
watching a blacksmith bend to them
in a forge in Terenure, and lift one and
fold it neatly over in his aproned lap
and touch the crescent foot
with a big file or pliers: the instrument
a glimmer in his blunt hand, the whole
horse-bulk rippling into shadow. A
few times, too, I felt tender rough lips
touch my hand that held, flat-handed,
a snatch of grass, fearing the teeth
but staying still until—grass gone
in a quick crunch—I had my hand back
to pat the silky nose, finger-comb
the mane, slap sleek hindquarters
and the belly big as a currach, to feel
the heat simmering there, the nervous
flickering along skin as if the veins
were charged, the blood itself electric,
and knowing how heavy the flesh was
from the way my hand lay on it
like nothing, a straw on water. I'd imagine

it all falling on me, or being lost
under a flail of hooves, the feel
of so much live involuntary flesh
capsized over my own bones
in a fury of bared gums, a trampling
froth-storm white at the mouth,
two black moon-mad eyes on fire.

2.

Remote, perfect, overwhelming
how they inhabit space
by crowding out the air they occupy;
and yet contained, confined inside
some glorious force field of their own:
a solidified smell of oats, sweat, leather,
contemplation, astonishment. The span
and ponder of them absolute
in anchorage, taut as propellors, steady
in that massive confidence of rump
and hindquarters, thews bulging, everything
sinewy, roped, rounded as sea-shells,
the grand parallelogram of the head
giving millstone definition
to the word *Skull*.

3.

Two white horses in a field up the road:
a mare and her colt gleaming
out of the clouded day, at grass
in a windless wide silence,
the tenderness between them palpable
as that mild and serious something

in an empty chapel. The young one
is lying down, while his mother
browses a close circle round him,
but when she stops to stare at
the sound my footsteps make
on the road beyond the hedge
at the edge of their world,
the little one rises too and stands
looking, his two coal-black eyes
lingering on my strange shape, letting
out of his lustrous ebony muzzle
a faint, plaintive, interrogative
whickering.
          I know they're abroad
in every weather—wind snapping
at all corners of the valley, rain-squalls
making ditches roar, sunshine
cooking the air in clover—and it is for them
only weather, to be taken
with the same dense patience
they proffer to whatever happens, although
at intervals under a heavy shower,
after they've been standing as still
as creatures carved in quartz,
the mare will suddenly toss and gallop
round the fuchsia-bush and barbed-wire
border of the field, her colt
quickly following, his new legs
slow and a little stiff at first, but then,
with a springy, kicking bound
and a careless, elegant animation
of everything that makes the body
and the body move, he'll cut
to a perfect dash, tuck tight

to a tandem gallop, doubling his mother
on the run—picking up as he goes
whatever he knows from her,
but first how to warm the blood
she's given him, and then
how to be, increasingly, in the world.

Swan in Winter

There is this enormous white sleep.
No marks visible on the soft body
sprawled on saltgrass in a few inches
of rocking water, the long neck
limp as water and flopping back
when you lift and let go, hauling it
out to the solid ground of shells
and seawrack, twilight lights winking
at the wide mouth of the Sound.

Orange beak, black legs and feet
blatant in that mass of white:
the lovely whole creature could be
asleep on the empty shore
in a settled silence dense with questions.
But you've nothing to say to this solid
apparition dropped from an iron sky
swollen with snow, the cold
biting through wool and goosedown,
the swan still warm when you
bury your bare hands in whiteness.

That such a great heart could stop
without a sign, those mighty wings
fold over one another for the last time
like that, the live body come to be
just a letting go in the cold, as easy
as entering at first the water, then
take hold of it taking hold and ride
the known currents, companionable
in the friendly element: imagine
those eyes closing, a deeper dark

than their own coming down, this
paschal candle of a bird snuffed out.

There is this solid feel of bone
inside the wing you've opened,
a hinged brightness wide as
a whitewashed wall, the life
seeped out of it, your own hinge-
winged hand the stronger, this huge case
hollow and heavy, immense, bereft,
but ruling in its white absence
the whole foreshore: it is its own
quartz grave, glittering as Newgrange,
and through it the old swan stories
come floating back, wings singing.

You twist with difficulty
one wingfeather out, pulling
until it comes reluctantly
to hand, lamenting the indignity
but wanting that unfading white
to keep catching light
on your windowsill, contain
this riddling death, this
inexplicable huge conclusion
from purely natural causes.
The quill weighs almost nothing
in your hand, the air in its shaft
electric, each ferny perfect barb
a lit shiver in the breeze.

Chill nips your naked hand
while this deep sleep suffers
no change, although every second
you expect a shuddering roll, the
sleeping beauty to stretch itself

under your touch, the knobbed head
jerk upright, those closed eyes
to open staring into yours
for a moment of pure knowing
as both of you say the one word, *Death,*
to one another, and it will wrench
its white tent of breath and blood
away, its force flooding back, the way

we want resurrections over
and over—of your father fallen back
on his hospital bed, his mouth
gaping after its last breath; your mother
cold in her padded coffin, cheeks
chill as glass, hard as bone;
or your friend sitting crosslegged
on the kitchen floor, a crooked
bloodstring hung from his nose,
hands held open in his lap as if
giving everything away; and you
waiting for their eyes to open
just once more, to say that
all's been known, all understood
at last, all taken in the one embrace
that is the whole body's grace and
affirmation in spite of all, as now

here, again, hoping against hope
the bird will wrench its bones away
and lean up, neck rising like some
great stalk, the head a blossom,
and flatfoot it cumbersome back
to water, wings flowering there
into full sail, and floating on the cold
until it feels fit to change elements
again, and will thrust, run, rise—

its neck riding the sudden loving surge
of air, and rising, *oh!*, off and away
into the surprised twilight like a white flame.

But of course it doesn't move
a muscle and you close home
its fanned-out wing and leave it there,
wondering what will happen next—
a high tide take it back, or gulls,
or the rats who inhabit holes in the rocks,
or crows strutting their live black
ravenous appetites all over
this white field.
                    Leaving as always
without answers, you see the inlet
lit up by three swans taking off
like gunshot, heraldic wings
hoarding all the light that's left
in the late day, letting you hear
the musical breath of their beating
as they pass over your head and
swerve inland, as you turn yourself
inland again, past the roofers' hammers
banging echoes up the wooded hill,
and past the redbellied woodpecker
glimpsed for an instant as it enters,
vanishing, a dead yellow locust.

At the Falls

Although the lilacs after all that rain have all
gone rusty, the sun's brought summer back
to warm your hair, and brings these three boys
down to the river where the cotton mill once
turned its big wheel, brings them to the flat
rocks at the falls where the swollen water—
colour of tin and tree bark—dawdles slowly
first in its approach and then plunges over,
its darkness transforming in an instant into
light and air as it twists like bolts of cotton
till it strikes the line of jutting rocks and
fountains down and out in a bristle-arc of
wet light, a flare of flashy water unwinding
to the bottom, where it goes on recollecting
the vertigo of its last moments aloft, the odd
exaltation of its fall as it leaped, wondering
would it ever be the same, the same again,
and breaking then into a hundred hands
of light, before feeling itself start to be itself
once more—slowed down, flowing away,
changed and not changed but held again
between sensible banks, and not a thing
of wings and terror till the next descent
narrows its throat and it takes the same rush
through its whole headlong body, ready
to cast itself away again, surrender
to whatever in its own nature keeps it
moving between such formless / formed
expressions of itself, until it loses all
its vast accumulated life to salt.
                              In khaki shorts,
the three boys gleam like sea beasts, making
their ungainly earthbound way over rocks
to step behind the water screen and stand there

in that numbing roar and reach their arms
out through it, stiff limbs hovering as if
disembodied, at odds with the steady state
of water-chaos that stretches back to when
first water began to make its creepy way
in the world, map the whole outlandish route
to its own undoing. The boys just stand there
in the deafening bliss of water—bodies behind,
arms in front, an image of its bottom line:
how it will not stay, how we are behind
and ahead of it at once—their young triumphant
flesh in water, who have not surrendered to, but
know, its near danger, *drunkenness of speed,*
the way it offers endless assent to gravity
by going over, going down, some of it flying off
as mist, pure spirit in the shock of boiling
almost against its nature, while the rest becomes
a heavy froth of light unfolding, struck thunder.
                                        And still
the eye's tugged back from what has happened
to what's about to happen, back to black water
with the luminous stain of tree bark through it
as it dawdles to the falls (*again!*) and then (*again!*)
taking the plunge, the rocks breaking it to brilliant
atoms of itself, another life if only for an instant.
Forgetful of their own flesh and pride of the flesh,
the boys stand still inside the noisy heart of water
and stretch their arms out, aiming crazy laughter
at each other, water striking and splashing
off their arms as if off fountain creatures
you'd stumble on around a cobbled corner
in Rome, and pause at the sight of the sleek
limbs of horses, thighs of gods, those glistening
torsos, nipples, fingers. Above the clamour
the boys are calling one another, convinced
they've entered and are at home for the moment

in the secret depths of this other element: still
the water won't stop and you watch it
refuse nothing, plunge and recover itself
from fall to fall, in terrible kinetic love with
gravity and going on, to rise somewhere
in fragrant dusk among jasmine and oleanders,
adrift, infinitely receptive and never-ending
like *the calamity of death*. It makes a music
you couldn't have intended or imagined, the ceaseless
stream of it brimming without intervals the air,
overflowing the ear, pure vigour taking its separate
self-absorbed life away in—always—the other direction.
                                             Now
the sun falls on the water and the arms projected
from the water, which will soon grow tired
of their own daring, this making strange of themselves
and the common element, and the sun falls
on your own head where you stand on the footpath,
warming your hair. As one who sleepwalks,
you sweat uphill again, find your way home
and fall into a deep sleep, your head become
one stanchless wound of sound and movement
streaming away, an opening to what could be
nothing but change, yet stands, a constant thing,
and flesh in the midst of it our signature saying
we belong, saying nothing stays.

Firefly

On my last night in the country, a firefly
gets stuck in the mesh of the windowscreen
and hangs there, revealing to me its tiny legs,
head like a miniscule metal bolt, the beige sac
jutting under its curl of a tail, splayed
on the fine wire and at intervals sparking,
the sac flashing lime-green, liquid, electric
—*on-off-on*, again *on-off-on*, then stop—
as if signalling to me in silence,
the trapped thing singing its own song.

For a while I watched it singing its own song
and then, when it went dark for a long time,
I leaned up close to the wire to become
a huge looming thing in its eyes and blew on it
gently, the way you'd blow a faint spark
to fire again—catching a dead leaf, a dry twig,
growing towards flame—and it started to flush
lime-green again, *on-off-on* again, deliberate
and slow, a brilliance beyond description
which filled my eyes as if responding to
the bare encouragement of breath I'd offered,
this kiss of life in a lighter dispensation,
as if I'd been part of its other world
for a minute, almost an element of air
and speaking some common tongue to it,
a body language rarefied beyond the vast
difference between our two bodies, both of us
simply living in this space and making
our own sense of it and, almost, one another.

It's how they talk what we call love to one another
over great distances, making their separate
presences felt in the dark, claiming whatever

the abrupt compulsions of the blood have brought
home to them, then seeking each other out
through the blind static that clogs up the night,
the mob of small voices and hungry mouths
coming between them, that grid of difficulty
they have to deal with if they want in every sense
to find themselves and decode in their own limbs
the complicated burden of this cold light
they've been, their whole excited lives, carrying.

Of course I don't understand their whole lives carrying
this cold light that might once have been a figure
for the soul, the soul at risk, worn on the sleeve,
its happenstance of chance and circumstance and will,
those habits of negotiation between its own
intermittent radiance and the larger dark; of course
the words I reach to touch it with are clumsy
and impertinent, nothing to the real purpose;
and of course it leads its subtle specific life
beyond such blunderings. But it was the smallest
of all those creatures I've come close to, looked—
however dumbly—into, and was still signalling
that last time I breathed its liquid fire to life,
blew my own breath into its brief body and it fell
from the wire like a firework spending itself
in blackness, one luminous blip of silence into
the surrounding night—the way a firework goes
suddenly silent at its height and drifts back down
in a dead hush, blobs of slow light growing fainter
as they fall into the flattened arms of the dark.

But for those moments it inhabited the dark
wired border zone between us, it seemed
as if it could be looking back at me, making
between my breath and its uncanny light
a kind of contact, almost (I want to think)

communication—short, entirely circumscribed,
and set in true perspective by the static-
riddled big pitch dark, but still something like
the way we might telegraph our own selves
in short bright telling phrases to each other—
on-off-on then stop—the whole live busy night
a huge ear harking to the high notes
of our specific music, and to the silence
that contains it as the dark contains the light.

Visiting Mount Jerome

1. *Alone*

After I'd touched down last summer on my parents' grave,
clutching yellow chrysanthemums and small carnations,
I wanted to walk away on my own at last, without
their gone bodies grappled to my tongue, wanted them—
when I stepped back from their names and dates—to stay
where they were together and, as the stone says, *At rest.*
I was waiting for a sign, a ghostly touch on the shoulder

or a voice saying my name, something abrupt and decisive
to take my bearings from, a sense of something—freely and
from out there—*offered.* Of course there was nothing in the air
except that silence that's the regional dialect of the dead,
their mother tongue, its one functioning tense an inexhaustible
infinitive we can't unscramble, and I knew I'd come to a
border as distinct as it's invisible, like the line that crosses

ordinary fields without a mark but is impossible to safely
step over, where we were to let go, take leave of each other,
or at least where they'd let me away alone and I would leave them
be as they'd become—their own completed selves at whose
unruly grave I'm staring, and staring with that puzzled look
of expectation and repose my own child had when I held her
for the first time and she looked into mystery, and it

was only me. All I could do, then, was turn from their stone
and move off among the other graves, remembering how, as a boy,
I'd be taken from them, waving, at the railway station, and how
I'd settle into myself for the time alone at school, something
winged with fright and exhilaration descending to nest in me

then, as it does now among the graves, when suddenly
and with not the slightest hesitation or strangeness I find

myself walking away, just like that, from my dead parents.

2. *With Youngest Daughter*

No candles, paper boats, nor any of the white acts of mourning,
only—diaphanous as a daylight moon—the dandelion clocks
blowing time away over the double grave we laid them in.

The place in disarray: one lumpy rectangle of dried earth
the width of a coffin. Hawthorn and chestnut in blossom,
Sunday figures afloat among tombstones, ablaze with

carnations, irises, chrysanthemums. I read their names,
the phrases chipped in stone, and she tells me
she can hear their silence, then straightens our two red roses

in a stoup of water. When we leave through the strait gate
of what was once an apple orchard, she takes my hand and says
If it starts to get dark or the path ends, will we turn back?

and before I can begin to imagine what she might mean,
a lark hurls itself into a spell of grace and improvisation
over our heads, rising for an age of pure song that keeps us

speechless, looking up, until it flutter-plunges into silence
and clumped grass, entering the aftermath as we two enter
the outside world, her warm small hand fiercely holding.

On Fire

How hungrily the wood grown light with weathering
burns, taking its own life till there's nothing left
but blackened fragments on a bed of ash, although it was
all sudden tongues and crackling at the sheer joy
of making its own unmaking like that, this perfumed, rash
expenditure of itself in a reckless cause. I remember
my granny's ramrod back in her widow's weeds,
on her knees in the hearth, bellows in hand, getting
redness to spurt among black coals. Or my mother
laying on their paper bed the sticks of kindling
I'd hatcheted from an orange-box that morning,
arranging the clinker remains of the last fire and
the gleaming nuggets of coal together, then quick
to the kitchen sink, stretching her stained hands
away from her apron. Or my father stacking turf-sods
in the dark mouth of the cottage grate: he'd get
the pale blaze going, then stand back to stare
and say, *There now*, with satisfaction, pour himself
a glass of whiskey, fold open the evening paper,
and sit into the old blue armchair we'd later burn
in the garden. Not discreet but daring, fire has its own
wild fling in the face of gravity, finding its wings and
not looking back, living brilliantly for the moment
it becomes nothing and a handful of ash. The ancients
saw souls in it with the heads of beasts, of birds,
and spent their lives handing it on, as we did
at dawn each Easter morning, quenching every flame
in the church and then—starting from the dark porch—
bringing the new fire into our lives, until the whole place
was ablaze and singing. Unknown soldiers of the world
have poured their own hearts into fire, while houses
of bricks and mortar, steel and glass, have curled up
in the teeth of it like leaves, and blown away. In love,
we are small gods shaking our sandals out as fire,

and at the end we may put our dead in it and gather up
what it makes of them—a few spoonfuls of speckled ash
and some bright purged bone. Its truest rhyme
is with *desire*—sprinting to touch, to act, all desperate
reflexive verb. Now the two of us here in the dark
have let the fire die slowly down, and it's your body
I want to see with the curtains open and the half-moon
pressed against the window—your long pale body
smouldering on top of the sheet, glowing beside mine
while we warm ourselves again in the heavy world
of matter, catching fire at the fire we make of our lives.

Ants

A black one drags the faded remains of a moth
backwards over pebbles, under blades of grass.
Frantic with invention, it is a seething gene
of stubborn order, its code containing no surrender,
only this solitary working frenzy that's got you
on your knees with wonder, peering into the sheer
impedimentary soul in things and into
the gimlet will that dredges the dead moth
to where their dwelling is, the sleepy
queen's fat heart like a jellied engine
throbbing at the heart of it, her infants
simmering towards the light. On your table
a tiny red one picks at a speck of something
and hurries away: one of its ancestors
walked all over the eyes of Antinous, tickled
Isaac's throat, or scuttled across the pulse
of Alcibiades, turning up at the Cross
with a taste for blood. In a blink, one enters
your buried mother's left nostril, brings a message
down to your father's spine and shiny clavicle,
or spins as if dizzy between your lover's
salt breasts, running its quick indifferent body
ragged over the hot tract of her, scrupulous
and obsessive into every pore. And here's one
in your hairbrush, nibbling at filaments
of lost hair, dandruff flakes, the very stuff
of your gradual dismantling. Soap, sugar, a pale
fleck of semen or the blood-drop from a mouse
the cat has carried in, it's all one grist to this mill
that makes from our minute leftovers
a tenacious state of curious arrangements—the males

used up in copulation, females in work, life itself
a blind contract between honeydew and carrion,
the whole tribe surviving in that complex gap
where horror and the neighbourly virtues, as we'd say,
adjust to one another, and without question.

Wet Morning, Clareville Road

Under morning greys of rain the roses
are washed, glowing faces, and in near gardens
the limp washing hangs with no hope
although all the slate roofs down Westfield Road
shine like polished chrome. Up early to make
a little door that opens out, a word passage
into the rain-filled air among the flowers
and the morning traffic—as if the words
themselves could offer light, could make
some sense of the muddle in which the heart
flutters. Dark green the overarching
ascension of trees; walled gardens
where scarlet roses are exploding; yellow
the cylinders of chimney pots; luminous
and edgy the fretwork clouds: how things
fall into place from a window, as if the given
were a pattern with precise meanings
and could console us for the loss of
signs, and spires, and words like *consecration*,
or could speak at least a little comfort
after sounding brass and after
the manic world where men go on
killing as usual, bringing lovely cities down
to rubble, dust. The town of minarets and bells
becomes a cry in the snipered street, hunger
a dog that howls all night, and out
among the hills not too far north of here
the consonantal guns and drums keep beating
and repeating their one word, while here
in our apparent peace there's nothing
but a wet hiss of traffic on glistening road,
the stark green shock of a privet hedge,
that bloodthirsty nude sunburst of roses.

If I went under the rain to smell the roses,
I would inhale your arms, the warm breath
between your breasts, the whole heady
exhalation of you moving by me on the stairs.
Is it because we can't hold onto something
as evanescent as a smell that—when it
finds us again—it brings the whole body
back into our ready arms, the steady undoing
of straps and buttons, cotton and silk things
drifting from our hot skin, a white shirt
forgetting itself awhile and flying
beyond its own down-to-earth expectations?
Shaken by a slight breeze, lace curtains
let light filter through to the room I can
only imagine, where a bowl of roses burns
on a low glass table by the window:
blue mutations agitate air, sea salt
stings the tip of the tongue,
and no ghosts but ourselves to stand
in that early play of light and its solutions
which may contain for the moment
time with all its grazing shades. The room
a flowering branch of details: this
brimming glass, this swimming mirror,
these peaches, this open book, this cracked
black and white Spode bowl, these trials of love.

When that space, with its shades of love
and its impossible colours, fades
to the wet morning outside my window,
I see only the tree in the back garden
bowed down as it is every summer
under a rich crop of bitter little apples.
But my brother makes the garden grow
once more, coaxing its flowers into the sun
like those unhappy patients he'll listen to

all day for their broken stories, crying out with joy
at the first start of the begonia
into pale pink blossom: *I thought it was dead,*
he says without thinking, *and now*
just look at it! He can talk of little else,
learning as he is not to grieve
but go on, and will—when he gets himself
out of bed this morning—fill the house
with his good will, looking forward
to whatever happens, ironing his shirts
to the sound of that soprano he loves
singing *Tosca*: when he thinks it's ready,
he'll test the hot iron as our mother would
with a spittled finger, then sing along as he listens
for the startled hiss that steams away
and, like a quick kiss, vanishes.

New Poems 1993–1995

I open the almond and its heart sparkles.
YVES BONNEFOY, "THE TOP OF THE WORLD"

One Morning

Looking for distinctive stones, I found the dead otter
rotting by the tideline, and carried all day the scent of his savage
valediction. That headlong high sound the oystercatcher makes
came echoing through the rocky cove
where a cormorant was feeding and submarining in the bay
and a heron rose off a boulder where he'd been invisible,
drifted a little, stood again—a hieroglyph
or just longevity reflecting on itself
between the sky clouding over and the lightly ruffled water.

This was the morning after your dream of dying, of being held
and told it didn't matter. A butterfly went jinking over
the wave-silky stones, and where I turned
to go up the road again, a couple in a blue camper sat
smoking cigarettes over their breakfast coffee (blue
scent of smoke, the thick dark smell of fresh coffee)
and talking in quiet voices, first one then the other answering,
their radio telling the daily news behind them. It was warm.
All seemed at peace. I could feel the sun coming off the water.

Place

First morning back, there's a faint cap of cloud
on the brow of Tully Mountain, flash of a blackbird
between sycamore and ash, glint of dew on a few daisies
the scythe has spared. Lilies of the valley stand

in a battered can, the cover of my mother's prayerbook
wrinkles with light, and my neighbour's rickety mutt
mumbles a crust of stale bread. In early sunshine
the houses across the lake seem solid as chateaus, seem

as if they'd stand forever: high-arched, their barns are
granaries of light, though the old cottages lie like bones
over the open fields. And here, slightly apologetic,
comes the cough of the cock pheasant, stepping

among potato drills as if he owned the place: crimson
and cinnabar his head, his feathers cinnamon and gold,
he will hide in his own life down there
where whins and heather and boggy grass can flourish

and the sunny morning be sheer heaven to him.

Sunshine, Salvation, Drying Shirt

Between the big window and the lake's blind flashes
I hang my line of Sunday washing—most of it grey
or black, one shirt ecclesiastical white, so you'd think
a priest was tucked away here off the beaten track
where—perched on the cross of the ESB pole—a kestrel
fills my head with Hopkins and his windhover
which I caught the other evening standing on air
unbuckled, almost stopped there, so I could spot
when the bird tilted—silhouetting itself—the crucifix
the poet must have seen, a sign bringing Christ
into the picture, causing the creature to buckle and
give off blood and fire, making a holy show of itself.

Flies hum, skiving a shaft of sunshine, and a chaffinch
dabs at the bread I shared with him for breakfast: could I
have been, I wonder, a monk of the Ninth Century,
my heart, too, in hiding, *stirred for a bird* and finding
God's fingerprints on everything? Drowsing outside,
the book of Basho fallen from my lap, I hear the note
a chaffinch makes breaking day in half, then gone, then
another answering with a little run of song, then silence
as the summer air lets go of them, teaching us how.
In his cell, the monk bends to scratch his ankle, watch
an ant at work, or opens the door to take the day to heart,
as, in a word-flurry, Father Hopkins blesses himself
before his bird can terminate its dive and take the life of
something hidden in the grass—a mouse, a lark—stabbing
through the neck and biting its head off. Meantime,

sun's a wonder on the back of my hand, my splayed shirts
keep shadow-boxing on the line, and a million midges dance
like dervish angels on a pinhead of light. When such days
stretch their slow-burning bodies out for us, it's hard to believe
the incredible weather won't hold up, as we want it to,

forever. But it won't, and even in the middle of its comforts
I know the flies gyring my head like atomies of air
would, given half a chance, make a quick meal of these
pulpy eyes. Still, with the last cleansing drop dripped out,
my clothes grow lighter in the light breeze, becoming
crisp as souls new-shriven, and from high in the heavens'
cloudless blue comes a twangy drumming as a snipe
shows off its climbing power—its silvered body all
bat-flap and ascension against the open sky—then turn
and curve, twist and fall, angling its tail-feathers to
make music from its own body falling like that, as if
singing the risk itself for the frightful pleasure of it.

Near Mount Kurokami, Basho changed apparel and his name,
then stood behind a waterfall and looked straight out
at what kept going. Next daybreak he was *off again
on unknown paths.* Here, pinned to its place, my white shirt
is all puffed up, I see, with its own radiance—a full sail
going nowhere—and in this silence that's come down on us
now towards evening like a cloud of light, the iron sound
of the Angelus bell beats round and round the valley.

Moment

Two small white butterflies settle
into their own moment, the male
lighting without fuss on the female
perched along the flat pink petals
of the cuckoo flower in the ditch
beside the road to Letterfrack, and she
holding on as he reverses direction.

How they take to each other, facing
opposite ways, green spines aligned
and delicately connected: his wings
fanned open, hers closed fast like hands
to show the frittillary intricacies
of the underwing, as if holding him
to an embrace that will let nothing

come between them. Quiet at first,
they suddenly flutter wildly for a few
long seconds, then quiet again until
a passing car startles and they
take off across the path of traffic,
still bound body to body as if
he's bearing her away, holding

at a steady height—her weight
his ballast, her wings still joined,
both absorbed in something more
than the species making itself safe
against the predatory crush and fuss
of matter—to land safely in grass,
gone from our sight. It must be

the subdued purposeful air of it all
that holds us, the way this act of theirs
shapes the world we share, spins
for a big instant the globe around
their truth against good sense and
judgement, the scandal of their sex
in tune with things, staining the day.

Unfinished

The house next door but one to this one
never happened, and all connected with its
shadow life are shadows now and maybe
tremble in the grassblades growing where
the planked earthen floor would have lain
between two walls facing east and west,
the front to where morning light still spills
over the bony shoulder of Diamond Hill,
the back taking in a flank of Tully Mountain
and the valley where the Atlantic evening
scatters its last handfuls. A half-built
shell of stone, it seems to stand as if
just broken from a dream, stunned,
its rags and tatters of raw stone
standing as a solitary gable, a single wall,
the big lintel-piece balanced almost on air,
the dead handiman having neatly slotted
stone to separate stone like the syntax
of a language that once trusted itself
and the sense it was making, left no gaps
of incoherence, nothing unsaid, knew
exactly how things fitted, could tell
the perfect place for any solid shape that
could be gathered from the field itself
into which it's lapsing now, a few
stones at a time, but mostly—in time
as we measure it—standing up to cows,
rough winds, persistent rain. I'm told
the man who began building left it as is
when the family of the wife he'd intended
denied permission. So he left and went
to America, they say, though no one knows
what happened to the woman. What
could her eyes have done, I wonder,

when she passed this way in the wake
of two cows, or going to Mass on Sunday?
I can't imagine the pause she'd make
on the far side of the sally bank, the drenched
fuchsia brushing her shawl, that gaping
half-made body looking blankly back at her,
and beyond it—through what would have been
their bedroom wall—the sheen of the lake
they'd have seen with some wonder
under a hundred lights. Somewhere
in Chicago or South Boston it may be
he tried a while to remember, or couldn't
help the hard walls his hands had put up
falling across his sleep, and then nothing.

I know the house I live in is—under its
whitewashed mortared skin—the same as his,
although it folded round itself, was finished,
and the weather that enters is a play of light
through glass, only the safe sounds of rain
on the roof or wind in the chimney. But
I love what he left, blunt masterpiece as it is
of understatement, its tight-lipped simplicity
getting the point across in its own terms
and caring for nothing but the facts
of the matter, the exact balance between
how this gesture registers in the world and
how the hard thing that happened, happened.

Six O'Clock

Steamy mushroom weather. Under the white pines
a smell of turpentine and dust. A young woman
swings by, her handbag the colour of ten-year-old claret.

In the cemetery someone is playing a mouth-organ:
There's No Place Like Home rises on the surprised air
while light-leaved saplings nod eager affirmatives

to each other (*yes yes, that's it, exactly*), stop a minute
to take things in, then again to affirmation.
I can smell the one pinetree cut down this morning

and carted away, leaving only this white stump of a thing
and its glimmer of dust, the lingering scent of resin. Airborne,
a glitter-flock of starlings expands, contracts, expands

like a beating brain, a heart pulsing, its every element
answerable. Our cat sees with her ears, each swivelling
to catch the drift of things on the breeze, as I go on

naming one thing at a time (*orchard, silo, hawk, eyelid,
sea-mark, bloody cranesbill, slate*) making windows
to peer into . . . exactly what? The hour that's in it?

Comet

Millions of miles above this road, this house
with sloping roof, garage, yellow maple,
it is arrayed in a white veil—a bride, a blur
of radiant gases, frazzled cloud around a fraught
blue heart of ice and electricity. To the huge
sound of it, thunder would be nothing, a lover's
whisper, although to us it is as silent
as the grave is, simply a sign in the sky
for itself, and I wonder what each of us
makes of it: the lucky conjunction it is—good
weather and moon-phase letting it through
to shine on us like this—or just a reminder
of onceness in the way things are, the way
at unthinkable speed it puts this world and all
its wriggling billions behind it—our native
maple trees, grains of sand, ants, riverbeds,
love-moans, death-rattles, shining eyes and
night chills—all behind it in its unearthly
tearing away, its headlong hurtleflight
and no return in time, in time
as we know it, no second chance for us
who are looking up this instant at
what happens, and passing with small
murmurs of satisfaction the binoculars
back and forth, trying to describe in our
own way, in plain words, what it is
we're seeing. In the end, Kira's shivers
force us indoors again, and we go back
across damp grass, sharing the good weight
of her between us, her white nightie
flaring behind—a trail, a bridal-train

to what she is for us who keep her warm
out of the breeze that ruffles her fair hair
and bundles up a glimmer-rack of cloud
to cover once more that sliver moon
and every other light in the sky.

Streak of Light

for Conor

After a party to celebrate the mid-term break,
you and your friends stripped after midnight
and streaked from one end of that great Lawn
to the other, from the dignified Rotunda pillars
to the bronze tip of Homer's nose, streaked
over the prospect Mr. Jefferson laid out
—who never imagined the moonlit spectacle
of six young first-year men in their pelts
flashing across the grass on goat-feet,
dashing to touch the poet's nose and back
over frosted grass to the steps, the safety
of their clothes again, breathless, the deed
done. Thinking about it, it's only *your* body
I see, and only in shrapnel flashes, the streaking
light of it on light feet, your red head
thrown forward, netting specks of moonfire,
the long strides and solid thighs of you,
stretched fingers tipping bronze as you turn—
a runner, something Greek—your sex chilled
by night and frost, but still in its strength
sending you headlong through the dark
like a cast spear in Homer, glimmering
and singing its flight. The moon
is remote, neo-classical, over where—
among the young men loudly hurrying
into their clothes—you catch your breath,
and I find, however it is, the rest of your life
branching from this rite of frosted passage, this
caper that stays in my mind as an image
of separation, the sight of your freshly stubbled face
alight like that, your vulnerable buttocks,
the fleet, gleaming ghost of you disappearing

through air the frost has turned to icy water,
and I stare—rejoicing as if I'd just hugged and
waved you off on some extraordinary venture—
stare after you, even after the night has done
what it has to do and swallowed you, even
after that last glimmer is gone from my eye.

Woman with Pearl Necklace

(Vermeer)

Since he painted her, she will always be putting this pearl necklace on
in her own ordinary room of light, the shaded yellow of it washing

to pure white where a wall becomes a painted nothing, a figure
for what he knew but could name no other way: the sheer intensity

of being this young woman this moment this morning, meeting
her own mirrored gaze, its marriage of modesty and rapture, and feeling

Me I am here it is I that is all I can see how they gleam how I seem
as her hands draw the ribbons that hold the band in place, fingers

lightly touching each other, the two hands between them seeming
to measure something—the weight the word 'soul' could bear, maybe,

to her eyes in the glass—the soul itself, it seems, assembled for once
on the very brink and fleshly lid of things, its mirror not the glass

nor the leaded window through which morning light finds her,
but that wall of all colours making white, which the painter faces.

Woman Sleeping in the Train

Her lips remind me of the mouth Bernini gave
Saint Theresa in ecstasy. Eyes not quite closed,
she barely breathes, and her head keeps falling,
it seems, over a wall of sleep, her whole body
suddenly one thing and open. Whenever the train
gives a sudden jerk, her forehead raps the window
and she opens her eyes, trying to bring things
into focus, then slides away again, and sleeps.

Small wonder the sculptor loved such a moment—
the complete surrender of it, a body hovering
between states, its spirit beating wings of light
and near flying—and set in stone the saint
giving herself to God, with God's young
pitiless angel grinning and levelling his spear
at her centre, her face naked and moisting over
with love sweat. But the woman I'm watching

is dry as a bone, a trace of pain in the way her mouth
stays slightly open, in which I think I see the remains
of something spent, let go. When she wakes at last
and looks out the window, all is commonplace
again, she an ordinary traveller as I am, nothing
rushing into her body and filling her to the brim
the way her sleep did and what went on in it—its
blind struggles of breath and flesh, its lick of fire—

and it's just the two of us looking through glass
in silence, like survivors, at the vanishing fields
and the light on the Irish Sea near Drogheda,

catching sight of our own reflected, reflecting eyes
as they catch and shy away from the sight of a man
pissing into a blackberry bush—head down, lost
in himself and his action—our tangled glances having
to take it and each other in as we look away.

Love Bites

As if they'd been walking in their sleep,
they've come through winter again, and now
the last stained remains of snow
huddle in patches, a whisper of ice may be heard
abandoning the windowpane, and three geese
are blaring from the cracked lake
their random fits and starts of jazz.

They've been asleep in different stalls:
while he nibbled the red, dust-scented straw
she mumbled her heartbreak into
the black glass of a Mexican choker.
Now days are thatched with light: they live
at first as if underwater, then terrible
air is storming their lungs and eyes.

Imagine being opened like a fish: the world
in front of your gaze a final time
and then nothing, namelessness, just light
slamming into broken rock, lives
silting together, lives in a heap,
the *lurching harmony* of things taking over—
as if we were creatures of hope after all.

In Late February

As when the siege of some great city lifts

and they sit outside on steps drinking hot tea
and making mindless chatter, I hear my daughter
after two months of snow and a sudden thaw
—feeling sun heat the hair at the back of her neck—
say the word *grass* over and over, seeing a strip
of pale green the robins are already mining.

Driving to work last Sunday, I thought the soul
might be a handful of blown snow, its scattered
shattered light vanishing before my eyes.
And yesterday, from a maple branch, I could taste
the barest trace of sweetness, encased
in a blade of ice where the branch had fractured.

Every night now, under the blazing stars
and over the ice cracking like toffee brittle,
a dog barks all night like my mind, keeping
the entire neighbourhood awake. But when
I meet the barefoot boy in the coloured waistcoat
walking home past midnight in a cloud of song

I know the old season is almost over,
and I almost love my own shadow again—
its attached levity making light of obstacles
and accelerating over known ground
like a catbird lost in the deep leaves of summer
but for its persistent, *pursue-me!* music.

Weather

After three or four days of persistent rain
something like panic sets in, a sense
of being smothered by wet noise,
nowhere to turn and nothing to be done
but hang on, hold out until some fresh
thing happens. I think of middle age like this,
when you can see bleakness
and no change, farther outlook only
more of the same, and you find yourself
saying this is the way things have to be
for good now. Even those you love
get stranger and stranger: you grow
more fragile with each other, thinking
of warm things in their burrows
who listen to the wind's loud mouth at the door—
how it bites and gouges all above ground.

But then the weather settles abruptly,
sudden as a reprieve, and that's the way
you could start to see your life—as if you'd
been let off again and not discovered
wanting. In the suddenly auspicious
light-breaking breezes out of the southeast
the sturdy panels of a well-made shirt—
white cotton drying on the line—seems
a hopeful canvas on which, between
now and evening, anything
can happen, wind filling the shirt-sail
with a fresh taste for adventure,
and even after eleven at night you can see
the pair of swans on the lake are two
incandescent glimmers of possibility
under a fitful moon, while the last
blackbird won't give in to the dark

but goes on, invisible as he is, singing
until your daughter wakes and says
Dad, I can hear the bird, it's laughing.
Is the rain all gone? And before
you can tell her how things are, she is
asleep again, and the house is spinning
its own sure silence round your lives.

Them and Us

In the hanging gardens of fuchsia and goldenrod
the moist air is a frenzy of insects

whose mouths gape, whose quick-as-a-blink sex
is sparking: furious, they seek peace, feel at odds

only with death, know the minutes they have
are all. When it's over, they drift into a sunbeam

and that's that. Our own stubborn dream of going on
has nothing to do with them, nor the word 'love,'

which is our way of conjuring any something
out of the air's empty sleeve: see how it hovers

in front of us now, lit up—a monstrance, or a lover's
mind-in-waiting while the station clock is ticking

towards the hour appointed, and away from it.

Martha's Vineyard in October

Noisy all morning under downpouring rain
are the upper stories of scrub oak and beech
and the bluejay with beaked acorn who stands
screeching on a rain-glazed porch railing
when the clouds thin and sunshine starts to stiffen,
making a breakthrough. They wake, rise and
move around each other, organise their lives for
a few days away: two families, grandparents, friends,
they mind the children, sit down to breakfast
with wet hair, three generations circling in surprise
to find themselves like this, intimate strangers.

In the poison-olive tree a cardinal snags a berry
and squinnies through the rain and glow of everything.
They see things in their hungers making do, and hear
the kids swapping curiosities: was that a whale
they saw, sudden island of dark on the bright sea,
breaching and disappearing and not coming back
no matter how long they stay peering out
over the tree-tops through the rain, seeing nothing,
yet still thinking *How well off we are*
here in this high sea-girt place facing south
towards shoals of light, invisible the next landfall.

Bullying its way beyond objections towards belief
his voice stops and listens a minute
to a whisk of rain against the kitchen window.
Guests arrive and the room fills with their voices
and his own, offering tea. In silence in the kitchen
he waits for the kettle of cold water to turn to steam, waits

for other devastating changes. Beyond the window
the sea is as Heraclitus saw it: *Half is earth*, he said,
and half the lightning flash. Now the light changes
and all things change in it: motionless behind glass
the children stand, making flames of their eyes.

. — — —

When brightness breaks up the rain, the place
swims in what they all feel but cannot call
blessedness, and before they start to speak again
they know, and are content to know, just the air
standing in a sphere of light, an embrace of airlight
taking all things to itself—trees, green openings of grass,
grey clapboard walls and gables, the biting colours
of chrysanthemums in a crystal vase, and in the distance
white slow-motion explosions where unheard surf
dashes itself, draws back, and dashes itself against the land.
The moment past, they fall to talk again. What happened?

. — — —

There is this simple fear that gathers in the gathering dusk
outdoors: light thickens in branches, and a last cricket
whistles faintly like a loved one's breath asleep beside you
in the half-dark—that you listen to for its sign of life, loving
its regular small presence and what it means to you, that leap
of faith it keeps making. But in this dusk he feels
the dying in things, feels a heavy thing without a name
grow slowly agitated—rising from the ground, pressing down
out of the air. And he wonders it could all *be* at all, and be
like this: this stew of smells, these unrepeatable crickets,
the dusk itself he stands in facing two paths, growing darker.

. — — —

Like ancient, sunburnt, nut-coloured refugees
the two crickets hobble into the middle
of the room the families have flooded with light
and look around them, making this low
whistling sound with their hinged bodies
until one of the children makes a false move
and they limp again into their familiar shadows
where they become the high-pitched
soul of the house, keeping the vacant place alive
through the dead season, this little glimmer
of music near the chimney while the snow rises.

The sun, on burnished wings, sweeps into the bedroom
and lights up half her face where she lies reading
a mystery, wondering how it will turn out.
When he sits down beside her, she raises her arms
to take him in, drawing his face to hers, his mind
lagging a bit aside from them and floating out
to where the waves glitter a persistent forced march
south towards the open sea, over which this morning
two dark arrows of geese went barking, that sound
bringing them to themselves from sleep, and covering
the true bed music they made as their bodies
became a small boat they tried to steady, staying here.

Drowsing in sunshine, she's on the edge of enlightenment
again, she thinks, but only sleep comes down
with its dream of surf breaking on sand, the way
each slate wave buckles and lets the light out
in a rush, then restores itself to dark water. He's afraid
for her in the force of the sea, that battering at sand

where a dozen sanderlings do their mechanical tango
with the lickety-split fringe of ocean: this is their world, all
salt and uproar, and they make a comic thing of it, unlike
how these two hold each other in the riptide—feeling
the ground give way, that felt solid where they stood.

A Life

All the way home, salmon follow their noses
up the old road, the known current taking them
to where they came from, where they will
disperse themselves to be the very element
they started from. This consistency of theirs—
faithful from wandering through the wide
open waters of salt, as if their whole life at sea
were a remembering and a looking forward,
something in the long glow of their bodies
on fire with this one spark, finding the right
artery and following it to the manner born
back to the heart that beats the future out
and stops—this deliberate existence of theirs
becomes a figure for us, its neatness appealing
to our appetite for design, and we forget
the long life they lead away from their
native place, the daily random and electric
adventure in the depths, the flickering shades,
twilight ringing and singing around them
its eerie high-pitched frights and assurances.
We forget how night plunges deeper and deeper
into water, their eyes seeking any crack
or sheltering crevice; forget the way they
twist their one bulky thrust of a body up
above the reefs as if they were flying; and forget
the music their gills make every minute,
filtering breath out of the heavy element.
Forget, too, the flattened conundrum of the net,
that perplexed ascension, our air throttling them,
dumbstruck glum eyes veined like grapes,
horrors of gravity, and the dark that takes them

—pursed to bursting with seed—into its own
unquestionable keeping, before they end up
on a white plate, slates of coral-coloured flesh
letting shrieks of steam out when you probe
that last lost succulence of theirs with your fork.

Summer Evening

A spear of zinc light wounds stone and water,
stripping the scarlet fuchsia bells and yellow buttercups

of any discretion, so they confess their end in this
luminous declaration that they are no more than

shortlived absolutes in living colour, bright eyes
open against the dark. A light in which everything

is exact-edged, flat, no bulk or heft to it, yet
decisively itself in outline: islands, the matte grey sea,

and miles away the fine glowing line of the horizon
that like desire will be the last to go. The mountain's

immense green and brown triangle reflects on itself
in lakewater, doubling its shape and colour there,

its stillness something drastic, an aspect of dread—as if
a lover tried to remember that loved other body

by looking in the mirror. Almost at random, shadows
fall across the small roads—which can never follow

their own bent, but always take the grain of the hill,
turning to its every tilt and inclination—and evening

starts to seep into hedges and hung washing: it is
the brown colour of a bat's wing, and silent

as a bat is. Even your own family now would have to
be streaked with it, their faces by degrees bleeding away

in the gather-dark, whole patches of them blackening
like zones of a map thrown on smouldering embers.

Bonnard, Daydreaming

Setting off without prologue or blessing,
you open the fish and put its bones on show:
somewhere between carmine and royal blue,
the flesh nestles between them.

Stone boats of Giza and Heliopolis
sunk in sand; the pyramids only teardrops
of stony light: you stand beside them
in your apricot frock, blocking each one out in turn.

Your shinbone makes the best music, hours
of the same song turning in my hand. Our daily life
is repeated over there: *Apricots, the whole tree*
glows with them, the dark leaves . . . . Over there

they hand out pomegranates, almonds, sweet figs,
cast a wooden flail after flocks of birds: their sky
is loaded with herons, moorhens, green pigeons
and what they call the laughing goose,

his black neck a shock on his white body. So
a comb matters over there, its tortoiseshell teeth
flashing in another light, and your hair matters,
and the curve of your back I've curled around,

and the cusp of tufted shadow that comes to light
when you bend over on the bathroom tiles,
the towel's white turban around your head
and under it the rest of you

smiling everywhere without a stitch on
here in the morning
before the world knocks, knocking us into
these whispers, pencil-thin, we live in.

Trip

Unable to change our bodies
into birds, we feel each pebble,
the pressure of every bend:
at blind corners we keep calling
Who's there? and run for it.

A snipe explodes against the bus window:
hard knock of the skull first,
then a burst of brown feathers.

Signs everywhere, but we go on,
your civil tongue in my head,
the mountain's back a ripple
under its skin of scutchgrass, your arm
weighting my shoulderblades, your cool
fingertips indenting my sunburnt neck.

Those great grief-carriers, the clouds,
are casting shadows
then wiping them clean
as we pass the clicketing sheep
who parade their speckled shins
and sooty kneecaps
through sepia light: from here
almost everything
will be under our breath.

We speed by a small shed
in flames: before we say anything,
it's ash.
Under your skin, in my hands,
your bones are burning. Later

you're cool as a handful of scallions,
your only warm part the tongue
in the live cave of your mouth,
its wet muscle
pulsing the way a shellfish must
just before it's opened, tasting salt.

Stop

We slowed and pulled over beside the body
on a side-road in the valleyed shadow
of two blunt hills near Sligo. With its
digger's claws, dust-encrusted pelt, a darkened
curl of blood between bared teeth, the creature
lay as if asleep, flies gilding it, when I stopped
the engine and got out to see my first badger,
a solid black and white case of absence,
and you got out too, took one quick look,
then walked ahead to the clump of bushes
briaring over a high bank, and leaned in
among the brambles (brown arms bare,
back straight, your left foot steady
on the verge, right leg stretched back
to balance you) and began picking
the fat blackberries, till you had enough
to bring two handfuls and spill them
on the flat dashboard, where they glistened
onyx and veiny vermilion when we
took them one by one and put them
in each other's mouth, splitting
each plump-fleshed bitter-sweetness
between our teeth, tonguing and swallowing
the dark ripeness of it. We drove on then,
the green after-rain peace of that deep valley
holding us a half-hour more
till we found the main road and turned
north on it into the thundershower
that would wash the badger's blood
away from our stopping-place, but not
the memory of it, nor of love
fenced round by barbs and brambles
yet flourishing among the fruits of the earth
and filling her hands for me.

Faith, Hope, and Danger

A small brown and gold moth
is lapping the living-room light-bulb,
who flew out of the folds
of my sweater this morning

like the soul, we've been told,
leaving the body
for free air and the fresh
perils of light.

I take note
of the cryptic signals
on its wings, their
hint of Aztec and Inca,

the touch of sun worship
about them, and of
its head that is all eye
absorbing a vast

acropolis of light
from the pear-shaped source
above me, the mystery
of which—being wrung

in the long run
from running water—
I've never begun
to fathom. Now

it has commenced
as I knew it would

kissing what fills it
with inexplicable hunger

and will any minute
fall, as we all do, from that
incandescent absolute
to the safe dullness of the rug

covering my writing-table—
where it will lie
stunned, wings shut,
until it rises again

a shriven angel
towards the light
that could be moving,
it must feel, the sun

and the other stars—
to fall near my hand again
and rise and fall until,
exhausted, I'll carry it

outdoors, lay it down
among fuchsia shades
where it can take
its chances in the dark

or towards dawn
in the real world
of beaks and talons.
When I wakened there

the other morning,
wondering what I was,

I could remember
nothing but the X-ray shape

of what I knew I had
run up against, a kind
of famished dazzle
and then blackout. Those

we call the Desert Fathers
had a word for this: think
of their long scouring
in the Egyptian sun,

how it singed them
to the bone as they bent—
light-headed from hunger,
hope and faith—over

the empty page, each
grain of sand a burning
word they sensed
but couldn't touch

with their tongues, each
insect noise or watery birdcall
or the ghostly
whisper of mothwings

in the eyeblink of dusk,
a soul-dementing
dear distraction
from the main business.

Couple on Park Bench

Back to back on a flat stone bench
they're at ease among the roses:
sun blanches the pebbled walks;
dusty pigeons nuzzle in sycamores.

The trees have lost half their lives
to the need for order, and make now
a neat avenue of shade
where couples with children walk

by an old lady feeding the birds,
murmuring their language. A jay
cries defiance from the shades
behind iron railings, and you might

for the moment be floating above
your own body, looking down
in late-afternoon leaf-filtered light
on this Etruscan couple crowning

their urn: she's raised her arm to point
to the way they bud and blossom
and blow their lives away, the roses,
in a fine riot of colour, while he

has fixed his gaze on the strictly
tethered fuchsia hedges, staked
at certain intervals along the borders.
Above, two pigeons are kissing,

necks wound round each other
like a capital letter in *The Art of Love,*

lidded eyes drowsy, indifferent,
collars shining in the green shade.

And caught in mid-stride, catching
both their eyes, a tall woman passes
in sunflower and crimson, her bag of blue
Italian leather jerking like a live thing.

Levitations

(after Chagall)

Airborne as they are, his lovers are solid as we are,
although we too drift between these walls of glass
as if we'd lost our moorings and might any minute
vanish through the skylight. They've lifted each other up
above the furniture with a single kiss, pointing themselves
in a westerly direction like two primed torpedoes,
or held together as halves of the one body, not yet
blown open and apart, their horizontal faces calm
and taking us in with little interest where we stare
from a net of blackbirds that pay no attention to how
we've stepped into the blue like this, hang-gliding
on our own updraft or doing the advanced backstroke
in our sleep. Coming back, we're groundlings, earthbound,
or you're upstream in a salmon jacket, me treading water
and snapping at the lure. Later, we held each other
in the palms of our hands and said, *Are we not*
light as feathers now, lying down? Here, then,
is the very self in all its cubist shreds and patches,
planted next to *The Poet at Half Past Three*, who is
a thing of stubble and vodka, cranberry atmospherics,
a crude rooster crowing in the corner of his eye
while his other half lies on grass, parcelled up in himself
like a secondhand violin and chewing a pointed leaf
of field sorrel, that cures thirst and putrefaction. Like us,
he is interested in the resurrection of the body,
wrapped as he is around a dream as hard as a barn door
through which the blue horse has just bolted. And now
we are coming in by the window again, bringing
my shoulders, your breasts and hips, a fan of black feathers
and a glass filled with, spilling, wine. Meanwhile an angel
on loan from Tintoretto makes a crash-landing
somewhere east of Kiev, translating the way the light

sits on things, all the realms of the lucid turned inside out
by this apparition of wings. His dog, it is true, barks
at the lilac tree, but the ground we think is steady under us
isn't, but spins its heartless wheel, while those savvy
whitebreasted swallows or sandmartins standing on the wind
like idle things, are all the time working their hearts out
to stay in the one place, still as we are, and go on holding.

Fenceposts

Inside each of these old fenceposts
fashioned from weathered boughs and salt-bleached branches
(knotholes, wormy ridges, shreds of bark still visible)
something pulses with a life that lies outside our language:
for all their varicose veins and dried grain lines,
these old-timers know how to stand up
to whatever weather swaggers off the Atlantic or
over the holy nose of Croagh Patrick to ruffle
the supple grasses with no backbone—which seem
endlessly agreeable, like polite, forbearing men
in a bar of rowdies. Driven nails, spancels
of barbed wire, rust collars or iron braces—the fenceposts
tighten their grip on these and hang on, perfecting
their art and craft of saying next to nothing
while the rain keeps coming down, the chapping wind
whittles them, and the merciless sun
just stares and stares: yearly the shore is eaten away
and they'll dangle by a thread until salvaged
and planted again in the open field, which they bring
to an order of sorts, showing us how to be at home
and useful in adversity, and weather it.

Papyrus

Acorn-brown, the girl's new nipples
draw the young men's rooster eyes
where a woman is fitting a man to her mouth,
breathing fire, holding for dear life.

Green almonds in their shells:
she knifes them open one at a time and
hands him a slick teardrop, cool white
tasting cool white. Nothing

compares with such austerities, although
the skull's honeycomb of bone
will break their hearts, who need hearts
like a bird's wishbone, to bend, unbend

at every feathery beat—wishbone hearts,
or something fleet and light as an ostrich's
leg-bone, bearing him to where, panicked
with grief, he can bury his head in sand.

Papyrus light: a scarf with black parrots on it
lifts in the breeze, and a real rare bird
is about to fly—his head in the clouds, his life
shrouded in daylight he keeps breaking.

Art

The whole chorus saying only one thing: look
at what goes, where we stand in the midst of it:
Golden eyes of the beginning, deep patience
of the end. Stone-deaf, the rocks in silence
are writing our lives: mossed, or lichen-daubed
to brightness, their gravity is here to stay. . .
but so is the butterfly winged with light
and in a dozen minds at once, letting its life
be wamble and whim as air determines, though still
a fixed purpose sticks to it, it knows the score
the chorus follows as one voice, singing
Light whelms, whelms, and will end us, while
a painter, old, is *leaning slightly to the right or left.*

Itinerary

Feel a passion for invisibility, be a fly on the wall,
the pitcher's ear, the child in the corner
with his eyes clenched. Like a dog going round
and round, you circle a space you've come back to,
trying to find some comfort, something that says
you're at home now. Pray for the enlarging hush
of the owl's ear, the hawk's high wide-angle lens
reading the world like a map. Your friend's
been weeding his potato drills. He stops and sits
on a rock for a cigarette. The sun has been shining
for days and days. *It's a gift*, he tells you.
A solitary thrush, with his heart in his mouth,
performs a dozen songs at dusk, none finished,
as if it were just himself and the world. Such
tense composure swells that speckled breast, warm
in late daylight: you see the beak open and close,
shivering into music. Wrapped in the spider's
winding-sheet, a bluebottle makes another music,
sawing the room in half: you note, till it stops,
each repeated live driving note. When you throw
open the door, the scent of fresh-cut grass swims in
and a huge yellow-edged summer moon hangs
alone in a powder-blue sky: a bright dense body
dependent on nothing. Stand back from nothing:
pussyfoot no more from the crux of the matter: you
must travel at the speed of light, not looking back.

Oasis

To enter this cool space
settles the stutter of nerves
that has taken your gaze
from the tall blue fall

of mountains in the distance:
you step into a ring of shade
in which you find this deep,
reflective, necessary source,

this simple joy
the committed body catches at
as if at the last gasp
of home: first the felt

luxury of shadow, its way
of slowing you down to know
what flesh is again, then
that sound the pool makes

stirring at its banks and
from the heart. *Water...*
you keep saying
its wedded syllables

as if they were enough,
their open and closing vowels
a cry before satisfaction,
though when you reach

its very self—the hard bright
splash of it—it's something
speechless, simply *known,*
the fluent pure give of it

first to the fever of your skin
and after
to that naive but greedy need
your tongue knows:

it fills, overspills
the heart in your mouth
like another life
gasping all its secrets at once,

and everything grows clear
as day breaking
through muslin curtains
to keep you here, where breath

swims in the saturated radiance
we came from, as if
two could go on saying
at the same time

the one good word.

Notes

Page 1: First epigraph: From a fifth-grade homework assignment done by my daughter, Kira. The crab is her own invention, although some of the facts belong to the behavior of a certain kind of desert-dwelling mouse.

Page 1: Second epigraph: "The Red Fern," from *Collected Poems* by Wallace Stevens. Copyright © 1954 by Wallace Stevens. Reprinted by permission of Alfred A. Knopf, Inc.

Page 12: "Tower House, Ballymoney, 1978": Part 3 was written much later than the other two.

Page 30: "Raeburn's Skater": The painting is *The Rev. Robert Walker Skating on Duddingston Loch*.

Page 40: "Traveller": The English explorer Henry Hudson thought he had found the chimeral Northwest Passage when he sailed up what is now the Hudson River. By the time he'd reached a point somewhat north of Poughkeepsie, he realised his mistake. The "wet sea-boy" is borrowed from Henry IV, Part Two (3•1•27); in some texts it is "sea-son."

Page 57: "Men Roofing": Chicago Hall is an academic building that houses the departments of foreign languages in Vassar College.

Page 65: "Conjunctions": The italicised phrase in Section 3 is from John Donne's *Satire III* ("On a huge hill, / Cragged and steep, Truth stands, and hee that will / Reach her, about must, and about must goe"). The Irish phrase *in áirde* ('erect') is from the children's song *An Maidrín Rua* (*The Little Fox*).

Page 85: "Sea Dog": Among the things in my head when I was writing this were Seamus Heaney's Bog Poems.

Page 87: "Rights": The line in italics is from a poem by Evgenii Rein, whose 1989 reading at Vassar College was introduced by Joseph Brodsky.

Page 107: "That Ocean": The figure of Peace appears in Ambrogio Lorenzetti's *Allegory of Good and Bad Government* in the Palazzo Pubblico, Siena.

Page 119: "Statue": A *kouros* in an exhibition called *The Greek Miracle: Classical Sculpture from the Dawn of Democracy,* at the Metropolitan Museum of Art, New York, 1993.

Page 122: "Women Going": Most of these figures refer to pieces of sculpture in *The Greek Miracle* exhibition.

Page 147: "Angel Looking Away": The pulpit by Giovanni Pisano is in the church of Sant'Andrea in Pistoia.

Page 162: "At the Falls": I believe the phrases in italics are from a poem or poems by Marina Tsvetaeva.

Page 187: "Comet": The comet Hyakutake could be seen in Spring 1996.

Page 189: "Streak of Light": On the campus of the University of Virginia, in Charlottesville.

Page 194: "Love Bites": *lurching harmony* is a phrase from James Gleick (in *Nature's Chaos*, text by James Gleick, photographs by Eliot Porter, New York, 1990).

Page 207: "Bonnard, Daydreaming": The italicised image is from a poem by Czeslaw Milosz.

Page 220: "Art": The italicised phrases are from, respectively, Trakl, Hopkins, and Cezanne. Cezanne's belongs to an observation he made in old age: "Here on the riverbank there are myriad subjects; the same view seen from different angles offers a powerfully interesting subject for study, and so varied that I think I could occupy myself for months without changing places, simply by leaning slightly to the right or left."

Acknowledgments

The poems in *Selected Poems 1978–1993* are taken from the following volumes: *What Light There Is & Other Poems* (North Point, 1989), *As If It Matters* (Graywolf, 1992), *So It Goes* (Graywolf, 1995). In Ireland, they were published by Gallery Press (*Wildly for Days*, 1983; *What Light There Is*, 1987; *As If It Matters*, 1991; *So It Goes*, 1995). The North Point volume contains the poems in *Wildly for Days* and *What Light There Is*, as well as a section of additional poems.

Special thanks to the MacDowell Colony and the National Endowment for the Arts.

And my thanks, again, Rachel.

Versions of the poems in *New Poems 1993–1995* appeared in the following magazines:

The Boston Review, "Papyrus"
Crab Orchard Review, "Unfinished"
Irish Times, "Art"
Janus, "Comet"
Michigan Quarterly Review, "Faith, Hope, and Danger"
The New Republic, "Place," "Summer Evening"
The New Yorker, "Couple on Park Bench," "Moment," "One Morning,"
    "In Late February," "Fenceposts," "Six O'Clock"
The North Stone Review, "Weather"
Open City, "Oasis"
The Paris Review, "Itinerary" (as "Traveller")
Pivot, "A Life"
The Plum Review, "Levitations," "Sunshine, Salvation, Drying Shirt"

Poetry, "Streak of Light"
Poetry Ireland Review, "Bonnard, Daydreaming"
Salon, "Trip"
The Threepenny Review, "Woman Sleeping on the Train"
Verse, "Them and Us"

I would like to thank the John Simon Guggenheim Foundation for a fellowship that supported the writing of many of the poems in this section.

EAMON GRENNAN is an Irish citizen and the Dexter M. Ferry, Jr. Professor of English at Vassar College. His previous books include *What Light There Is & Other Poems, As If It Matters, So It Goes*, and his translation, *Leopardi: Selected Poems*. Grennan is the recipient of a Guggenheim and a NEA fellowship. His work has appeared in many Irish and American journals, including the *New Yorker, Poetry Ireland Review*, the *Nation, Poetry*, and the *Threepenny Review*.

Relations has been produced for Graywolf Press at Stanton Publication Services, Inc., in Saint Paul, Minnesota. The typeface is Legacy, designed by Ron Arnholm. Legacy reinterprets Renaissance masterpieces for digital composition. The roman is based on a type cut in Venice by Nicolas Jenson around 1469. The italic is based on letters cut in Paris by Claude Garamond around 1539. This book was designed by Wendy Holdman. Printed by BookCrafters on acid-free paper.